AMERICAN SPAZ
THE NOVEL

Greg Kieser

Copyright ©2011 by Greg Kieser

All rights reserved under International and Pan-American Copyright Conventions. Published in the United States by American Spaz Creative, Brooklyn, NY, and, simultaneously, in the United Kingdom and Australia.

ISBN: 978-0-9839842-2-1

Cover Art by Faydzul Muizza
Back Cover Photo of the Spaz hand is by Felicia Kieser
Inset photos of Spaz are from the short film "How I Became a Spaz"
Photo of Bob Kieser Sr. is courtesy of Bucks County Courier Times
Cover Design and Layout by Greg Kieser

Principal Editor: Alex Amerman
Editors and Readers: John Guare,
Marna Poole, Devvon Bradley and Michael Tighe.

American Spaz is a work of fiction. All of the characters, incidents, and dialogue are imaginary. Any similarity to real persons is coincidental and not intended by the author.

For

Mom, Dad, and Beth

and

Bob, Cathy, Joe, and Brian

CHAPTER 1

"Dad's going to die," Mom told Henry.

Dad was there, and so were Henry's three older brothers and two older sisters. They all waited for Henry to react, but he didn't. He just sat there, watching the sun pour in through the stain-glassed windows of the old wooden church. It was a Saturday afternoon and the pews were empty, except for the eight Kreisers.

"We wanted to wait until we were down here at the shore to tell you," Mom continued, "so we could all be together in a peaceful place." She took his hand.

"Why is everybody staring at me?" Henry asked, looking at his brothers and sisters.

They remained quiet to allow Mom to respond.

"God will protect you," Mom said. "You know that?"

"More important than that," Dad spoke up, "is that you be strong about this."

"Can we go fishing now?" Henry asked. He stood and walked out of the pew.

His brothers and sisters all glanced at each other, confused by how quickly Henry changed the subject. They filed out of the pew behind him.

The Kreiser family walked out of the church, an old gray wooden structure that faced a sand dune and the ocean beyond it. On either side of the church were cottages and small beach homes in greens and blues. Their rental cottage was set back from the beach a few hundred yards tucked into a thicket of Jersey pine trees. Henry ran ahead, up a path over the dune. "If we use the squid," he called back to them, "we can catch the big fish, right?"

"Nah, clams should work fine for bait," his eldest brother said, as they all ran to catch up to Henry.

Their fishing poles were leaning against the dune fence. Henry grabbed his, a smaller one, while Dad and the brothers took the bigger ones.

"But the man this morning caught that big fish with squid." Henry said. "Didn't he?"

An elderly woman sitting in a folding chair watched the Kreiser family walk across the beach. It was clear to her that Henry was the youngest of a big family—a slight boy with bleached-blond hair. She inspected the others, trying to figure out their ages. The next oldest brother had red hair. Then there was a dirty-blond brother, a redheaded sister, and a dirty-blonde sister. The eldest brother had shoulder-length dirty-blond hair and kept his eye on Henry. Dad was clean-shaven and had darker hair, pale skin, and wire-frame glasses. They were a slender, fair, blue-eyed bunch. Mom saw the woman watching, so she gave her a polite nod and looped her arm in Dad's, as they continued across the beach.

All eight walked in silence. Mom stayed close to Henry. When they passed over a jetty, a World War II bunker came into view. It was a massive concrete structure that sat on the sand partially in the surf. On top of the bunker, fishermen tended to their rods. Henry ran ahead to the bunker and climbed the steps while his brothers and sisters followed him. Mom paused on the sand, taking hold of Dad's arm. "Wait."

"What's wrong?" Dad saw a worried look on her face.

"Don't you think it's strange?" she asked.

"What's strange?"

"The way Henry just ran out of the church after we broke the news to him—like it was just another day."

"He wanted to go fishing. I don't see what's wrong with that."

Mom paused and thought about it. "I don't know. I just think—"

"Don't worry. He'll be fine." Dad went up the steps

onto the bunker. After a moment Mom followed him.

Over the course of the next couple of hours, Dad and the boys baited their lines. They cast them repeatedly as Mom and the girls watched. A few fish bit, but none were hooked. Then, as Dad pulled his line in to wrap up, Henry yanked his own fishing rod suddenly. "I got one!" He yanked again, jerking the line with a sudden sense of panic.

"Calm down!" Dad placed his rod down to watch Henry.

Henry jumped in the air every couple of seconds in an attempt to get the upper hand on the fish. His brothers started to laugh, but Mom and his sisters exchanged worried looks.

Mom leaned over to Dad. "Help him."

Dad shook his head. "No. He goes crazy like this every time—exactly when he should be staying calm. He has to learn."

"Learn?" she said quietly to Dad. "Don't you think he's acting out now because of what we just told him."

"Henry, calm down," Dad called. His brothers wanted to help him reel in the fish, but Dad motioned for them to stay back. Henry yanked the line again. Then, he was reeling it in quickly when it got jammed, so he began spinning it frantically in the opposite direction. The line made a hissing sound and quickly bundled into a bird's nest as the reel locked. Henry glanced at his brothers, and then at Dad. "It's stuck!" he yelled. He threw the fishing pole on the ground and grabbed the line, attempting to pull the fish in by hand.

"No, Henry!" Dad yelled. "You'll rip your hand apart!"

Dad picked up a filet knife, grabbed Henry's rod, and slashed the line, cutting the fish free. "Now it's going to die!" he told Henry then tossed the knife aside.

Henry watched the line fall over the wall and into the ocean. His face froze in horror for a second. Then he turned to Dad with hostility. "He's not going to die!" Dad moved to embrace Henry, but Henry dodged away and ran down the steps. They all watched from the bunker as

Henry began walking along the beach.

"Henry!" Mom yelled. "Henry!" She turned to Dad. "Can you go get him?"

"I'll go," the oldest brother said.

"No. No," Dad said. "I'll get him."

Dad followed Henry down the beach, but Henry walked fast enough to stay ahead of him at first. Then, Dad sped up. Henry glanced back as Dad caught up to him, and then stopped. He sat on the sand.

Dad sat down next to him. They had reached the southernmost point of the cape and were looking west across Delaware Bay. They watched the small bay breakers as the sun neared the horizon.

"What was Mom talking about before, Dad?"

"When?"

"At the church, she said you were ... going away."

Dad saw Henry's lip start to quiver. He slid over on the sand and wrapped his arm around Henry's shoulders, feeling them tense up at first then slowly relax as Henry unwound. After a moment, Henry dropped his head in his hands and sobbed. He blubbered unintelligibly about the fish that would die from the hook in its mouth.

Mom came over and sat on the other side of Henry. He wiped his tears away and sniffled as she put her arm around him. After tying off the rods and cleaning up the bait, the others also trickled over. As dusk arrived, the Kreisers sat there, quietly huddled together on the beach, leaning into each other with Henry, Dad and Mom in the middle. They stared out over the bay, watching the last moments of the sun and letting the sound of the crashing waves make them numb. The elderly woman who watched them cross the beach earlier that day now walked by behind them with her chair.

When they got up to return to the cottage for the night, Mom grabbed Henry. "Stay here for a second. I want to talk to you."

Dad and the others started back.

"Tough times are coming," Mom told Henry, after the others were out of earshot. "That goes for you *and* your brothers and sisters."

Henry looked at a lone ship light on the dusk horizon. A few stars speckled the darkening sky above it. He nodded.

"To survive tough times you need to remember very simple lessons—love God, treat people with respect, be good to yourself. And family, Henry, always rely on your family. We're all here for you."

"Okay."

"Are you listening to me?"

"Yes."

"Look at me," Mom said, touching his chin. "You have a big family, you know that?"

Henry looked at her. He watched the evening breeze toss her hair and saw sincere concern in her eyes.

"Henry, would you give me a sign that you're listening, please?"

He nodded. "Okay." The sorrow that had gripped his face when he first sat on the sand with Dad was gone now.

"Okay?" Mom asked.

"Yeah."

* * *

That was the summer of 1978 in Cape May Point, New Jersey. Henry Kreiser was seven years old; his oldest brother was seventeen. Summer turned into fall, and fall turned into winter. Henry celebrated his early December birthday like any other eight year old. Then a car crashed on a snowy night, just days before Christmas. It was the winter solstice—the darkest day of the year.

On New Year's Day, the six Kreiser children stood around a hospital bed in the intensive care unit of Mt. Holly Hospital in New Jersey. Dad, who was the center of their attention, seemed suspended above the bed, tangled in tubes and wires and wrapped in casts. Their grandmother and her husband, Mr. Cluskey, entered the room, unnoticed by the Kreiser children. A woman in her mid-sixties, Grandmom wore a brown waist-length sweater, while Mr. Cluskey, a slightly older man with a paltry patch of white hair, wore a plaid suit. Grandmom wiped her moist eyes with a tissue and led Mr. Cluskey off to the side of the room, giving the children space to be with their critically injured father.

She looped her arm in Mr. Cluskey's. "I'll need you to be flexible in the coming months, dear," she said.

Mr. Cluskey examined the Kreiser kids. "How so?"

"At the very least, they'll need our support and guidance as their father recuperates. But maybe they'll even need…" A tear rolled down her cheek, so she dabbed it with her tissue.

"They'll even need what?" he asked, putting his arm over her shoulder.

"Who knows? Maybe they'll even need to stay with us. What happens when a family loses their mother?"

A few weeks later, Dad's eyes opened suddenly. All six of his children were around his hospital bed watching him. Most of the tubes and wires were gone. Dad blinked his dry eyes for several moments and looked at each of them. "Where's Mom?" he asked.

Henry and Byron were swept out of the room immediately by the two middle, early-teen siblings, Teddy and Liz. The two oldest, Kate and Chuck, stayed in the room with Dad.

"She … passed. She died in the accident, Dad," Kate said gently.

"What accident?"

"You were in a car accident," she took his hand in hers. "You were driving."

"I was driving… where in the world… why are you am I?"

"Huh?" Chuck asked. "What are you trying to say?"

"Driving world where was I?" He stared at Kate and Chuck for a long moment.

Kate sighed. "Dad? What are you—" Before she could finish her question, Dad's eyes closed again; he slipped back into unconsciousness.

The Kreisers lived in suburban Levittown, Pennsylvania, in a one-story, green, asbestos-sided house, pretty much like all the other houses on their street and the streets beyond. It was in that house, a month later on a Saturday morning, that Dad woke to a home-cooked breakfast. He was disheveled but had a sideways smile on his face, and his eyes were full of energy. Henry's two oldest siblings, Kate and Chuck, made scrambled eggs, bacon, and pancakes. Dad ate himself full without saying much.

Mom's seat at the opposite end of the table was empty, but otherwise everything was normal. On the wall behind Dad was a photo of the whole family dressed in their best—Mom, Dad, and all six kids. "Sears" was stamped in the corner in gold print.

After his third cup of coffee, Dad sat back in his chair and released a long sigh. He smiled at his children. "Guess I should get myself back to work," he said. He looked at the crutch leaning against his chair, and his smile faded.

"I forgot to tell you," Chuck said. "They called yesterday."

"They called?" Dad asked.

"Yeah, they wanted to know when you'd be back."

"Yes. That's what I'll do. I'll get back to work." Dad glanced around the room then closed his eyes for a moment. When he opened them back up his face hardened in seriousness. "But before I do that, we have to get this house back in order and solve some mysteries." He turned to Chuck and Kate. "You two are the oldest. I want you to take on some responsibilities. You both can drive, so I want you to start searching the surrounding area immediately."

Chuck and Kate looked at each other—confused. "Search for what?" Chuck asked.

AMERICAN SPAZ

Dad didn't answer. He pointed at the two middle kids, Liz and Teddy. "You two can keep the headquarters stocked with rations and prepare meals for the troops." Dad got up and grabbed his crutch. He hobbled over to the two youngest, Henry and Byron. He leaned against their chairs and put a hand on each of their heads. "And you two will keep headquarters spick-and-span."

Before anybody could protest, Dad left the room, his crutch knocking on the floor with each step. "Get to work!" he called over his shoulder.

They all sat there, not sure how to react to Dad's sudden volley of instructions.

"What's he talking about?" Teddy asked.

Chuck motioned for them all to gather close together. "He's having trouble accepting reality and he doesn't remember the car accident," he whispered, "so we should just play along for now."

Teddy began welling up with tears. "Well, he's supposed to be helping *us*, not us helping him. I'm not playing along!"

Henry searched the face of each of his brothers and sisters, trying to comprehend their discussion.

"Just play along Teddy," Chuck insisted. "Please!"

"Why?" Teddy asked. "Tell me why we should."

"Because Dad just needs some time," Kate said. "If we give him some time and be slow and loving with him he'll eventually see the truth. He'll see that Mom really is gone."

Chuck nodded his head. "I think that will work and we need you to cooperate." He glanced at Henry and Byron. "We all just need to stay calm."

"No," Teddy said. "We need to confront him right away."

"I agree with Teddy," Liz said. "Let's just tell Dad to snap out of it."

"Kate and I are the oldest," Chuck argued. "We'll make the final decision."

"No!" Teddy stood suddenly. "I will not pretend Mom is alive when she's not." Teddy knocked his chair over as he left the dining room. When he rushed into the hall that led back to the bedrooms he nearly bumped into Dad, who had snuck up to listen to their conversation. Teddy ran into the nearby den.

Rain began to fall that afternoon. Liz and Teddy hid in the den and demonstrated their defiance by playing records as loud as the record player would allow. They played rock ballads and southern rock anthems. Both Kate and Chuck stopped by the room multiple times to tell them to turn it down, so the noise wouldn't anger Dad, but the rebellious teens ignored the advice every time. Henry poked his head in the room at one point and saw them standing near the window smoking cigarettes. He found them silent and staring off in different directions as they released long puffs of smoke that only partially made it out the window. A cloud lingered above the spinning record player that jammed with an extended guitar solo. Despite looking off in different directions they were standing shoulder to shoulder, leaning into each other and didn't seem especially approachable to Henry. He quietly closed the door and walked away.

Rain continued into the evening. Kate and Chuck prepared spaghetti and meatballs while Byron and Henry set the table. Smelling dinner, Teddy and Liz wandered into the living room and flopped onto the couch.

"Let's go!" Chuck called as he entered the dining room with the pot of spaghetti. Kate followed him in with a bowl of meatballs and a container of grated cheese.

"Where's Dad?" Henry asked, as they all sat down.

"Somebody go—" Kate began to say, then stopped when she heard Dad's crutch knocking on the floor as he approached.

They grew quiet as Dad negotiated the space between the chairs and the wall to go to his seat at the head of the table. They saw his face still hardened in seriousness.

As dinner began nobody uttered a word and remained tense. Halfway through dinner, Dad slammed his cup down on the table suddenly, and all six of them nearly jumped out of their skin.

They saw's Dad's face contorted in anger. "Where's my wife?!" he demanded, his accusatory eyes searching their faces one by one. Henry turned away when Dad's prying eyes reached him. "I have the feeling your grandmother is hiding her somewhere," Dad continued.

"But Dad!" Teddy jumped up, slamming his fist down on the table. "Mom passed away!"

"Oh," Dad channeled his anger at Teddy, "suddenly you know everything!?"

"I know that—"

"No! You don't know anything, so don't act like you do," Dad argued. "People lie! Your grandmother lies. The newspaper lies. Your mother is alive, and we'll find her."

Teddy ran out of the room while the others sat frozen in fear.

"I want all of you in the living room tonight for a discussion about this," Dad demanded. He grabbed his crutch and got up, leaving his plate half-full of spaghetti. He limped over to a nearby glass hutch and moved some plates from the top shelf. As they watched him, he pulled two rifles out, tucked them under his arm and left the dining room.

"What's he doing with the guns?" Kate asked Chuck. She stood and nervously glanced out to the hall where Dad went.

"You two," Chuck said to Byron and Henry. "Take your plates to your room and stay there."

In their bedroom—a converted garage with three little windows—Byron and Henry finished eating, and then sat on their beds. Neither spoke a word as they listened closely for any activity elsewhere in the house. Outside they heard the rain pelt the window. After a half-hour, Henry felt his head begin to throb in mild pain, so he lay back and looked at the ceiling. His mind wandered and entered an open space with blue sky, far away from where he actually was in that moment. In minutes he dozed off.

He woke up more than an hour later with the throbbing headache stronger now. As he opened his eyes, his vision blurred for a moment before it cleared up and the ceiling came into focus. Then he heard yelling. It was Dad. "Where is she?" Henry heard him yell. He sat up, gathered his senses and glanced over to the other bed. Byron was gone. When Henry heard Dad scream the same question again, he darted for the door. But when he twisted the doorknob, it wouldn't open, so he threw his body against it. He felt it rattle, as if it might open, then threw his body against it again. The second time he hit it, the door slammed open with a bang. A chair, which had been placed against the door to lock him inside, fell to the floor.

Sneaking into the dining room, Henry climbed under the table and peered into the living room between the legs of a chair. He saw Dad pacing on his crutch, so he shuffled on his knees to get closer. His five brothers and sisters were standing in line, at attention. The ache in the back of Henry's head pulsed again, and his vision blurred. Dad's head hung low as he searched the faces of Henry's five siblings. Henry saw Dad engaging them in the same accusatory manner he used at dinner. But now Dad's aggression was punctuated by fleeting moments of vulnerability, when he cast his eyes down and became disoriented. In those moments Henry began to well up with sympathetic tears. But, when Dad revealed his aggressive side, Henry felt no sympathy. Henry saw Dad turn to the couch to look at something. The two rifles were there. For a moment, Henry thought there were four, but he looked closer, squinted his eyes through the spindles of the chair, and confirmed two. When he tried to get an even closer look, he banged his head on the bottom of the table—a sound he was sure they all heard. Byron did hear the bang and turned to see his little brother under the table. He motioned for Henry to go back to the bedroom.

Kate and Liz sobbed.

"We told you, Dad," Teddy said. "She died in the accident. You were driving!"

Henry heard a sharp smack. He looked through the spindles of the chair again and saw that Teddy's face had a red handprint across it. Teddy stood in shock. Henry felt his own face flush in confused anger. The ache in the back of his head pulsed, and his vision blurred again. Dad's unpredictable movements made him appear as two people for a moment. Henry squinted so he could watch Dad closely.

"Why'd you do that, Dad?" Teddy burst into angry tears.

"I did that for whatever you do wrong in the future. Now I asked a question, and I want an answer. Where'd you hide my wife?!"

"She died!" Chuck exclaimed. "She was in the car."

"Stop it, Dad!" Kate yelled.

"What don't you understand?!" Chuck stepped forward. "You were driving!"

"You're crazy!" Liz screamed. She grabbed Byron to take him out of the room, but Dad raised his hand and she froze in fear.

When Henry saw Dad raise his hand again, he scrambled out from underneath the table, knocking the dining room chair over. He ran into the living room and approached Dad with ferocity, as if he was going to attack him with his little clenched fists. But when Dad reared his head and shot Henry a threatening look, Henry, too, froze and moved to stand next to his siblings. Dad became quiet. He picked up one of the rifles, fidgeted with it for a moment, then sat on the couch.

As the mood softened, Chuck stepped quietly next to Dad. "We told you, Dad. You were in the hospital for months. You were driving the car when Mom died. It was snowy night in New Jersey. You hit a tree."

"You just want to blame me," Dad said, barely audible.

"No, we don't." Kate approached from the other side. "It's the truth." She looked at the rifle in his hand.

Dad studied each of their faces carefully—searching for signs of betrayal. Chuck reached to take the rifle out of Dad's hands, and Dad slowly released his grip. But when Chuck gently pulled away the second rifle, Dad looked up suddenly. "Put those down!" he demanded.

Chuck returned the rifles.

Then, Dad pointed at Henry. "Are you on my side, Henry, or on theirs?"

"Wh-whose side?" Henry asked.

"The others," Dad reached for Henry. "Them or me?"

Henry evaded Dad's reach. "I ... no. Yes. I don't know."

"Well, you have to take a position! Do you want to see your mother again?"

Kate took Henry in her arms. "Leave him alone! There are no sides. How could you ask him to choose between us?!"

Dad didn't say another word that day.

Henry woke in the middle of the night. On the other two beds in his bedroom, he saw Byron and Teddy sleeping. Henry got out of bed and walked out through the kitchen into the girls' room. Liz slept with a baseball bat at her side. Kate curled tightly under the covers. He continued to Chuck's room. Chuck was asleep, fully clothed, on top of the covers. A velvet jaguar poster glowed in a black light. Henry heard a shuffle in the next room— Dad's room. It seemed Dad was the only other person awake in the house, so Henry approached the door and listened. He was about to walk away, then he heard a drawer slide shut and sniffling.

"Dad?" Henry called. He knocked lightly on the door, and then pushed it open. Dad was sitting on the bed. Henry looked in Dad's eyes but didn't see an ounce of the anger or aggression that he had seen earlier. He saw tired, helpless eyes that had been crying. Henry sat next to him. Dad put his arm around Henry's shoulders.

Henry let out a long sigh. "I miss Mom," he said.

"I do too, Henry. More than I have ever missed anyone."

When Henry woke in the early morning, he realized he had fallen asleep on the bed next to Dad. He got up quietly and left the room. He wandered through the house, feeling like he was awakening from an emotional fog, as if he was beginning to more fully comprehend what was happening. In the living room he examined the furniture and pictures on the walls, but then his gaze caught the family portrait that hung on the wall in the dining room. He squinted his eyes and tried to focus on the faces in the portrait, but from that distance, the only definitive shape was the frame. He took a step forward and squinted again. Still it was all a blur. Intent on seeing the family picture with clarity, he approached the wall and climbed up on a dining room chair.

Kate walked in from the kitchen and found him there, with his nose nearly touching the portrait. "Why are you up so early?" she asked him.

Henry looked confused. "When I was standing back there, this picture was a blur."

She held two fingers up. "How many fingers do you see?"

"Four."

"Henry! What happened to your eyes?"

"I don't know." He climbed down from the chair and touched his eyelids with his fingertips.

Kate took a step back and held four fingers up. "How many do I have up now?"

He squinted for a moment. "Two?"

A week later, Henry was sitting in the living room with his brothers and sisters. He had glasses—big plastic frames—on his face. He was still adjusting to them, so when they slid down on his nose, rather than pushing them back up, he tilted his head at the oddest of angles. He examined his siblings with his new vision.

Henry saw Teddy watching Kate and Chuck suspiciously. Then he observed Kate and Chuck exchanging secret glances.

"What's going on?" Teddy asked them.

Chuck paused and looked at the younger boys. "Bad news," he said.

"How could things get any worse?" Teddy searched Kate's worried eyes.

"It's gonna get much worse. We're gonna lose the house."

Greg Kieser

Henry finally pressed his glasses back on the bridge of his nose so he wouldn't have to tilt his head. He sat up straight. He looked at the family picture on the wall, seeing every detail now, even his mother's pearly smile.

"If we lose the house," Teddy asked, "where are we gonna go?

CHAPTER 2

"She's got a luxury car and a luxury husband," Dad said to the kids, as they all gathered around him looking out the living room window. They watched as Grandmom walked up to the house with Mr. Cluskey.

A bit later Grandmom and Mr. Cluskey sat at the kitchen table with Dad, Chuck and Kate. "I appreciate your generosity," Dad told Grandmom. "But this is my family, and we'll get through these difficult times. We don't need your money."

"But where will you go when you lose the house next week?" Grandmom asked.

"We'll figure it out," Dad said firmly.

"With no money!?"

"We don't need money to survive! We have resources. We have each other." Dad got up to leave.

Grandmom shook her head in dismay. "I'm sorry. My daughter didn't raise these beautiful children for them to be abandoned by their father. I'm going to have to—"

"What are you going to have to do?" Dad said, his eyes challenging her to continue.

"I'm going to have to ask the state for permission to take them away."

Dad stared down at Grandmom and then over at Mr. Cluskey.

"I'm just here to help," Mr. Cluskey said, shifting in his chair nervously.

"Out," Dad said, pointing at the door.

AMERICAN SPAZ

"We ... you ... listen, please," Grandmom tried to explain.

"Out!"

Over the next few days Kate and Chuck secretly made plans for the family. And, while Liz and Teddy knew they were up to something, Dad, Byron, and Henry didn't have a clue.

Three days later, just before daybreak, Grandmom and Mr. Cluskey pulled up to the house and waited in their car. Chuck and Kate came out the front door with Byron and Henry and a few bags of clothing.

Teddy came out in his pajamas, followed by Liz, and saw Kate rushing Henry and Byron into the backseat of the car. Kate kissed each of them on the forehead and closed the car door.

"Where are you taking them?" Teddy yelled. He and Liz ran toward the car, but it began to pull away.

"Drive," Mr. Cluskey ordered Grandmom, looking over his shoulder at Teddy and Liz approaching the car. "Drive!"

Just as Teddy reached for the door handle, the car sped off.

As they pulled away, Henry and Byron watched through the back window. Henry was startled to see Dad come out of the house in his underwear and pull Teddy inside by the collar. Kate, Chuck and Liz followed them inside.

Henry leaned up to the front seat. "Where are we going?" he asked, glancing to see if Byron knew something. They were both welling up with tears.

"You'll stay with us for bit," Grandmom answered.

"How long?" Byron asked.

Mr. Cluskey turned in his seat to look at the boys. He was visibly upset and had a drop of sweat on his forehead. "Not long," he said, wiping his face with a handkerchief.

That afternoon, at Grandmom's house in Magnolia, New Jersey, the boys were exhausted—emotionally and physically. The old-people pace of life was evident immediately; it was torturous and magnified their pain. Just to take a pee Henry waited thirty minutes by the door while Mr. Cluskey flushed three times and exited the bathroom slowly with a newspaper tucked under his arm. The boys scrunched their noses at the smell of mothballs. Henry sat uncomfortably on the Victorian furniture. Byron flipped through *Reader's Digest* under a lamp made of purple glass.

A sunny, late afternoon lunch was prepared—peanut butter and honey on white toast. Grandmom and Mr. Cluskey sipped Lipton tea. Two poodles, one black and one white, sat at the foot of the table. Mr. Cluskey took his tea into the living room and sat down at a Wurlitzer. He began playing a happy song and singing for the kids. He smiled gaily at them with an air of pomp.

"He does that on TV, boys," Grandmom said. "Have you ever seen the Al McCain show?"

Henry nodded. He spread peanut butter and struggled not to tear the toasted white bread.

Mr. Cluskey looked into the kitchen at Henry and stopped playing suddenly. He walked over and grabbed the knife from Henry. "That's not how we spread, Henry. It's like this—across the bread. Spread evenly so you don't break the bread."

For a moment Henry stared at Mr. Cluskey standing above him. "Okay," Henry said, turning to Grandmom, "I want to go home."

"I'm sorry, dear. You can't."

"I. Want. To. Go. Home." Henry stood.

"Shhh," Byron said.

"*I want to go home!*"

"Grandmom," Byron said. "Can you tell us what's gonna happen? When are we going home?"

She took Byron's hand in hers and pulled Henry over by her side. "I don't know."

* * *

Henry and Byron settled in at Grandmom's house. Weeks passed, and boredom rose. Light summer evenings gave way to cool autumn nights. They started classes at a new elementary school. As the trees began to shed leaves, Henry spent hours looking out the window. A bare sky let the cold light come.

One Saturday, while watching kids on their bikes from the living room window, Henry took his glasses off, put them on the coffee table and walked outside to make friends. Over the course of the following weeks, he befriended two boys in particular—a pair of twins, named Ron and Don, who were the biggest kids in the pack of mostly eight to ten year olds. While the twins systematically trained the other kids in their pack to respect their rule, Henry was in no mood to be bossed around, and he invariably stood up for himself. As a result, in a short amount of time, he became one of the top dogs.

On the day before Halloween, Henry put his eyeglasses on the coffee table and yelled from the front hallway, "Going with Ron and Don to the woods!" He ran out the door.

Grandmom went to the living room window and watched him walk off with the pack of boys. She noticed them all looking around and conspicuously passing something back and forth. Worried they were up to no good, she decided to follow. She grabbed Henry's glasses from the coffee table, took her jacket, and ran out. She followed the pack of boys down the street and into a nearby wooded area, where she hid off behind a tree. She saw no inappropriate behavior and started to leave. But then, a puff of smoke rose into the branches above the boys—and another soon floated slowly upward. When she took a closer look now, she spied Henry taking a long drag of a cigarette. She headed down the path towards them immediately. On seeing Grandmom walking rapidly down the path all of the boys escaped into the surrounding woods—except for Henry, who, without his glasses, didn't see her coming.

He blew smoke. "Where you guys going?!" He coughed repeatedly then turned to see Grandmom was just a few yards away. Henry froze, with several smoldering cigarette butts at his feet. She grabbed him by the collar and slid his glasses on his face.

Back at the house, Henry was seated at the kitchen table with a pad of paper and a pencil.

Grandmom looked down at him. "Henry! You are on a very bad path. Do you realize that?"

He nodded his head.

"One hundred times. 'I will never smoke again.'"

After Grandmom left the room, Mr. Cluskey came in. He watched Henry begin writing and shook his head in disapproval.

Henry shook his head too and mimicked Mr. Cluskey's pursed lips sarcastically before he started writing again.

Mr. Cluskey leaned over and whispered in Henry's ear. "Your mom is rolling over in her grave. Do you realize that?"

Henry froze and put down the pencil. As the words echoed in his ear, they seared the image on his soul.

Henry barely spoke a word in the following weeks. He avoided all contact with Mr. Cluskey. At church on Sunday, Henry and Byron sat on either side of Grandmom. Along with the congregation they got up, they sat down, and then they kneeled and got up again. Henry sang the hymns mechanically. Then the priest released the incense—frankincense and myrrh. Henry sniffed. It provoked a memory; his mother's coffin there. He looked to the front. The image of her rolling over inside of it tangled his imagination in knots and stole his breath away. He shook his head to make the image go away. He pushed his way to the aisle, knocking a woman back in her seat, and ran outside.

When Byron came out, Henry was sitting on the steps. And then Grandmom came out. "Let's go," she demanded, heading for the car.

AMERICAN SPAZ

On Thanksgiving, Kate came to take Henry and Byron for the day. They drove across the bridge to Pennsylvania to Kate's new home in a three-story brick apartment complex—a sleepy community, with blinds pulled. Trucks and vans lined the lots.

By late afternoon, the table was set. Kate lived there with her boyfriend, a reddish-haired Irish guy named Jack. All six of the Kreiser kids were together again. Chuck's girlfriend, Veronica—an alert, smiling brown-haired girl in a mini-skirt—sat back and watched their banter. She was amused to see familial sarcasm and pranks begin.

Teddy pulled Henry out of his chair. "Stand here." Teddy handed Henry a quarter. "Hold it out."

"Why?" Henry took the quarter cautiously.

"Just do it." Teddy turned around to face away from Henry. "I'm gonna try to grab it from your hand. You have to try to pull it away before I do."

Henry focused and prepared, flinching with Teddy's slightest movements. At the very moment Teddy swung around, Henry yanked the quarter back and screamed. "I won..." But, also at the very same moment, Byron, who had snuck up, yanked down Henry's pants and underpants. They slid over his skinny hips with ease and fell to the ground. Henry stood frozen for a second, bottom nude, before falling to the ground and pulling his pants up.

"No," Byron said. "You lost."

Kate and Liz, immune to the comedy, shook their heads. But Veronica nearly fell out of her chair in laughter.

At dinner, they had all of the standards: mashed potatoes, candied yams with orange and lemon slices, and jellied cranberry sauce with wrinkles from the can. Kate delivered the turkey—a plump bird modest in size. "My first turkey," she said. "Dig in!"

Jack carved the turkey. Oohs and aahs sounded out as the plates filled up.

"This turkey is *so* moist," Veronica said. "What's your secret?"

Midway through the meal, Henry, who had fallen quiet, nibbled on a slice of orange from the sweet potatoes. "Where's Dad," he asked.

All fell quiet. Kate looked to Chuck and then to Byron and Henry. "Dad lost the house."

"So, where is he?" Byron asked.

"Remember Mr. Watson?"

"The ice cream man?" Teddy asked. "Great—Dad is living with the ice cream man while we have to live all over the place."

Kate shot Teddy a look. "He offered Dad a room," she said. "We should be thankful."

"Can we go see him?" Henry asked.

Kate shook her head. "No. I don't think he's in the right condition."

"But I'd like to see Dad," Byron said.

"Yeah," Henry said, "of course. Can we go after dinner?"

Kate and Chuck exchanged glances. "They should be able to see him," Chuck said, "even if he's not in the best shape."

Henry finished his dinner quickly; he ate too much. By the time the pie was served, he had his jacket on. "When are we going?" he asked, as he scooped cherries out from underneath the crust of the pie and piled them into his mouth.

Henry and Kate sat in the front seat of the car. Byron was in the backseat. They pulled in front of a white suburban house on the edge of a wooded area. Several broken-down cars lay falling apart in the overgrown grass.

Henry opened the door to get out but Kate stopped him. "I have to tell you guys something" Kate said. "Dad is sick."

Henry nodded. "We know. He doesn't have too much longer to live. Right?"

"No. I mean he's sick in another way. Like the way he acts might seem strange."

"What do you mean?" Byron asked.

"The doctors gave him pills to make him act normal, but he doesn't take them. So he may... he may act strange."

Byron leaned up from the backseat and tapped Henry on the shoulder. "Remember when he had us all lined up?"

"Yeah, I remember," Henry said.

"Another strange thing is..." Kate said, putting her hand on Henry's arm, "is that he only likes to see one person at a time. Go ahead in that side door and up the steps. It's the first door. Make sure you knock. And bring this to him." She handed him a plate covered in tin foil. A turkey leg poked out one side of it so Henry pushed it in as he took the plate. But then a chunk of sweet potato fell out from the other side and onto the floor of the car.

"Don't touch it," Kate said. "You're making a mess."

Henry went into a dark hallway. At the top of the steps, he found the door and knocked.

"Just a moment," Dad called.

Henry looked around the hallway. He heard a man snoring somewhere farther down the hall.

Dad opened the door. "Come in." Dad's room was small—single bed, orderly desk, stacks of paper, pens and pencils in a mug. "Welcome to my home, Henry." He pulled a chair out from the desk and sat on the bed. "It's not big, but it's comfy. How's life with your grandmother?"

"Okay." Henry looked at the stacks of paper. The handwriting was neat and lengthy. He picked up the top sheet. The page beneath was the same. Then he picked up the next. The pages were full of handwriting. He began to read to himself from the fourth page. *The problems of society lie in the inability of people ...*

"Just okay?" Dad asked.

"What?"

"With Grandmom. Just okay?"

"It's good, I guess." Henry sat on the chair.

"Do you like her husband? Mr. Cluskey?" Dad asked.

"I hate him!" Henry's eyes flashed with anger.

"Why?"

"I just hate him." Henry shrugged. "That's all."
"Well, you should tell me why. Did he hit you?"
"No."
"If he hit you, just tell me. Okay?"

Henry shook his head, and then got up from the chair and looked out the window. Then he looked at his hands and twiddled his fingers.

"What's wrong?" Dad asked.
"Just thinking."
"About what?"
"About what you do," Henry answered. "About what we're gonna do."
"I'm trying to finish my writing, and then I'll find a job."
"Dad, please ..." There was a faraway look in Henry's eyes. "Please get a house and bring us back together again. Please."

Dad stood. "You know they say I'm going to—"
"Die," Henry interrupted.
"Yes."

Henry nodded. "I know. That's why I want to ask if me and Byron can come stay with you."
"Stay with me?" Dad looked around at the small room.
"Yeah. We're small."
"I don't think they'll let you. I lost custody."
"Well, I want to. I'll convince them. Do you want us to stay here with you?"
"Of course! You're my sons!"

Henry stared out the window at the trees—all gray trunks and branches with no leaves. Then he realized he could see the former Kreiser home through the yard of another house. He saw a man, woman, and child going into it. He turned his head down suddenly. "Who lives in our house now?" he asked Dad.
"A family."

On a Sunday morning, Henry was playing Monopoly with Byron when Grandmom walked in. "You're both going to church," she announced. "Put your suits on."

"But we're playing," Byron said.

"I don't want to go," Henry said. He jumped up and ran outside.

Henry lay back on the front lawn in front of the evergreen hedges and stared at the sun. He opened his eyes wider, feeling the intense discomfort deep inside of them and resisting the impulse to close them. Finally, when he could see no more, he flipped over and put his face in his hands.

When Henry entered the church that morning, he grabbed Grandmom's hand. With the disk of the sun burned on his eyes, he could see very little. His eyes adjusted as the service started, but the orb still floated wherever he looked. Then the smoke of frankincense and myrrh arrived and evoked images of Mom. He followed the orb through the smoke. Sunlight poured in through the stained-glass windows. He imagined his mom by his side. The priest chanted, looking to the sky. Dizzy for a moment, Henry was about to sit down when he experienced a sensation of absolute clarity. He felt a connection with something on the other side that pierced him deep inside. And when the call to prayer silence came, he dropped to his knees in the pew. He threw his face in his hands and prayed to the Lord recklessly. He shed tears and blubbered his prayers. A lady in front of him turned and looked back in dismay.

"Silent prayer," Grandmom whispered to him.

* * *

Henry threw himself at the feet of the Lord, praying every night and going to church willingly every Sunday. He stopped playing with Ron and Don and the other neighborhood kids altogether, and he never took his eyeglasses off again. He did well in school—marveling at geography specifically. Like church, it made him feel like he was a tiny part of something great and wide.

Grandmom was proud of him. But he never forgave Mr. Cluskey. And every opportunity he had to agitate the stodgy, older gentleman, he did just that. He found it easy. And he took pleasure when he saw Mr. Cluskey turn sour. He and Byron stayed with Grandmom and Mr. Cluskey in New Jersey for two years. But the elderly couple had not planned on raising two boys at that stage of their life.

One afternoon, in the fall of 1982, Byron sat in the living room, trying to hear what Grandmom was whispering into the phone. She seemed to be plotting and planning a complicated operation. Mr. Cluskey sat in an armchair nearby reading the newspaper. Henry, who was eleven years old now, took the top off a crystal bowl of chocolates. He searched through them and put his teeth in one. He poked it with his tongue to taste it but then put it back, adding some theatrical flourishes to get Mr. Cluskey's attention. And then he did it again.

Mr. Cluskey caught Henry's prank out of the corner of his eye and put the newspaper down. He gasped as he got up and grabbed the bowl. Then Henry snatched it back.

"Incorrigible!" Mr. Cluskey wagged his finger at Henry. He called out to Grandmom, "He's biting the chocolates and putting them back. His mouth on every one!" Mr. Cluskey grabbed the bowl back again and went to the kitchen where he put it on the top shelf of a cabinet.

Henry spotted a cigarette lighter next to a candle so grabbed it and ran outside.

Byron followed him out. "Where you going?" he called as Henry ran down the street. Byron followed Henry for several minutes but intentionally left him some space. When Henry entered the woods Byron lost him for a moment, so he ran into the woods to search. A minute later he caught up with Henry on a path next to a small clearing of dry, knee-high grass. Byron stood behind a tree and watched Henry pull out the lighter and flick it repeatedly. When Henry held the flame to the grass Byron jumped out from behind the tree. Henry blew on crackling grass and a small fire started.

Byron ran and pushed Henry down; then he stamped out the growing fire. Henry got up quickly and darted to the other side of the clearing and lit the grass again. And Byron ran over to him and pushed him down again. But this time a breeze whipped at the fire. It crackled across the dry, grainy grass tops and quickly became too big to stamp out. Byron grabbed Henry by the collar and pulled him out of the woods.

As they walked back out to the street between two homes, Henry broke free and ran ahead.

"You're an asshole!" Byron yelled.

"Cluskey is an asshole!"

"No. You are!"

"Well, he's the one that convinced Grandmom to get rid of us."

"What are you talking about?" Byron asked.

"I heard him tell her we have to go! What do you think she's been doing on the phone?!"

Byron stopped trying to catch up to Henry and followed him back to the house.

Thirty minutes later, Grandmom was still on the phone in the kitchen. In the living room, Byron and Henry watched through the front window of the house as a fire truck sped past with lights and siren blaring.

When Grandmom got off the phone and entered the living room. She pointed to Henry. "Sit down there on the couch with your brother. We have some things to discuss."

Henry sat down. "I didn't do it," he declared defiantly.

"Didn't do what?" Grandmom asked.

"Light the—"

Byron coughed, interrupting Henry. "He didn't do the dishes. It was my turn."

Grandmom was confused. "Okay, don't worry about the dishes. I have some news for you. Things are going to change and you have a choice to make. A family you know wants to adopt you both. But it means your last name will change."

"I'm not changing my name," Byron said. He looked to Henry. "We're not changing our name."

"Don't decide yet. That's the first choice. The second one is a boarding school in Hershey, Pennsylvania, near the chocolate factory. It's for kids from difficult situations."

"Can't we just go back to Levittown?" Henry asked.

"No, Henry, I'm sorry. I need you to both think about these two choices and give me an answer by tomorrow."

Both Henry and Byron lay awake that night.

"Byron," Henry called.

"Yeah?"

"Who do you think wants to adopt us?"

"I don't care." Byron sat up in bed to look over at Henry. "We're not changing our name."

"So, where do you want to go?" Henry asked.

"The school. The one in Hershey."

"Me too," Henry said.

The next morning at breakfast, Henry searched the table—orange juice, white toast, butter, and wheat cereal. "Where's the sugar?" he asked.

"Sugar makes kids bad," Mr. Cluskey said. "If you can't handle chocolates you can't handle table sugar."

"What'll it be, boys?" Grandmom asked. "Did you think about it?"

Henry spread butter on the toast unevenly. "What about our family?" he asked. He jabbed the knife and ripped apart the bread.

"I'm so sorry this is happening to you. But, as you know, your dad is sick and your brothers and sisters are too young to care for you."

"The school in Hershey then I guess," Henry said.

"The school," Byron agreed.

"I think it's a good choice." Grandmom gave them each a warm nod.

"Yes. Some discipline," Mr. Cluskey said.

"It's beautiful." Grandmom put a hand on each of their shoulders. "Really beautiful. The rolling farmland and barns. You'll even get to milk cows when you get older."

"Really?" Byron asked. "Cows?"

"And roller coasters. There's an amusement park nearby."

"Cows and roller coasters?" Henry asked.

CHAPTER 3

Grandmom and Mr. Cluskey drove the boys away. From the backseat, they watched their life pass from the suburbs to a rural, open space. They stayed quiet. Henry slumped, put his feet up, and looked at the November sky. Clouds were high but thick and dark. He cried quietly against the window. Byron tapped Henry's elbow. "That's life," he said, shrugging his shoulders. Henry looked back out the window.

Two hours after they started, they turned off at the Lancaster exit. In Amish country, they passed slowly around a horse and buggy. A bearded man with a black hat held the reins. Henry looked up at the man and saw him staring peacefully ahead. He poked Byron. "He's looking at the horse's butt," Henry said. Byron laughed. Henry laughed too, but then stopped suddenly.

"We're arriving in Hershey, boys," Mr. Cluskey held his hand up to get their attention.

Henry stuck his tongue out at Mr. Cluskey. Grandmom caught Henry in the rearview mirror and shot a look.

"Here's the chocolate factory," Mr. Cluskey continued.

Henry nearly leaped into the front seat to get a look. Brick buildings were six stories and windowless. Smokestacks sat idle. Hedges in a flowerbed spelled two words: CHOCOLATE TOWN.

Over the railroad tracks, there was a park full of amusements: a coaster with loops, another wooden one, a log flume and a swing ride. The tops of the rides were visible over vine-covered fences. The park was quiet and closed for the season. On a golf course, a lone man swung a club. Farmland opened. Corn stalks were broken.

Then, as they came over a hill, a massive, white marble, domed building came into view. All four of them leaned forward as they took in the sight. The countryside around the domed building pitched and rolled. They could see dozens of farms and basketball courts on the hills. Sprawling homes sat among patches of autumn trees.

"Wow," Grandmom said. "It's stunning."

Henry and Byron each stared out their windows. Byron tapped Henry and smiled. "It's nice, isn't it?"

Henry nodded.

In a brick building were the administrative offices. They waited and then went in. They sat across from a suited man seated quietly behind a desk. Stacks of paperwork obstructed Henry's view. After a long silence the man pushed the stack of paper aside and leaned back in his chair. "I want to tell you young men a little story." He looked at Byron and then at Henry, who was fidgeting with the armrest on his chair. "Are we paying attention?" the man asked.

Henry sat up in his chair.

"Milton Snavely Hershey," the man started, "one day dedicated his milk-chocolate riches to white orphans."

"Orphans?" Byron asked. "We don't ... we are ... we have a dad."

"Understood. It was an orphanage in the beginning. But, lucky for you, modern times led to widening the acceptance policies. If a child needs help, we are here to help. Girls and all ethnicities are now accepted too. You'll see Hershey had a great idea. He built farms to instill a work ethic in the students. Cows need to be milked twice daily—every day, three hundred and sixty-five days per year."

Byron milked a cow in the air. Henry almost smiled.

Forms were filled out. Dotted lines were signed on.

Outside, dusk had fallen. A yellow streetlight shone down on the car. Grandmom became pensive and misty. "I wish I could do more," she said. She gave two kisses on two heads. Henry hugged Mr. Cluskey but crossed his fingers. Soon, Grandmom and Mr. Cluskey were on their way and Henry and Byron stood on the curb with the suited man. They watched Grandmom's car pass between two fields, under a streetlight and out of sight.

An extraordinarily long station wagon, one that looked like it could carry twenty people, arrived to pick them up. There were so many doors that Henry and Byron struggled to choose one to get in.

"You can sit in this first door," the driver, an elderly man, called, pointing to the first row behind his seat.

Henry sat up and folded his arms on the front bench seat as they pulled off. "Are you taking us to the chocolate factory?" Henry asked.

The driver shot him a grumpy glance. They passed a wide two-story school building. On the other side of the school, student homes were set back far from the road among darkened cornfields. Through the window of one home, Henry saw a bunch of girls gathered on a couch. The station wagon passed a pond and went up a long slope alongside a patch of stately evergreen trees. Where the road flattened out, it ended with a small traffic circle that the driver negotiated with the long station wagon. When the car came to a stop the Kreisers beheld the name of their new home. On a wooden sign was painted "Moldavia". A long walkway lined with young trees curved up to a sprawling ranch-style home that was fronted by a long porch. After the boys were dropped off with their bags, they spotted a man and a woman come out the front door on to the porch.

"Is that them," Henry asked.

Byron started up that path. "Yup. Let's go and get this over with."

Henry followed several steps behind.

"Byron Kreiser," Byron said, extending his hand as he arrived at the porch. "Nice to meet you."

"Mr. and Mrs. Kerning," the man said. "We'll be your house parents." The Kernings were mid-fifties and lean.

Her reddish hair was permed and perfectly round while his hair was parted on the side and neatly combed.

Henry stayed back. He nodded and extended his hand to shake only after they offered theirs to him.

Inside, thirteen boys were lined up, waiting to greet Byron and Henry—white boy, white boy, black boy, Latin boy, and more white boys. All were clean, well groomed, and dressed in slacks and button-down shirts—pale yellows, blues, and greens. Byron worked the line and shook hands. "Byron Kreiser; nice to meet you," he said. "Byron Kreiser; nice to meet you."

Henry followed behind but wasn't as gregarious as Byron. He only extended his hand when another boy did so first. Then he grabbed it, squeezed hard, and let go quickly. They all shook Byron's hand but a couple of the kids saw Henry's hesitation and didn't extend their hands. When they reached the end of the line, Mr. Kerning indicated the place they were to stand with a sweep of his hand. "Welcome to Moldavia," he said. "You'll see; a fine place."

A blond boy tapped Henry. "We call it Mol*slavia*," he whispered with a slow country drawl.

Mrs. Kerning shot Henry a look. She walked in front of the row of boys. She straightened Henry's shirt and nudged his foot back with hers. "Stay in line," she said. "And all will be fine. We run a tight ship here."

When the other boys were excused, the Kreiser brothers were asked into the office. The Kernings laid out the rules. "Listen, obey and don't lie. Do your chores right or action will be taken. With the others, have respect, don't touch their belongings and don't call them names or action will be taken."

Henry stood in a daze. "What do you mean, action will be taken?" He looked on the wall behind Mr. Kerning where a wooden paddle hung.

Mr. Kerning turned to the wall. He looked at the paddle. "There are many different forms of punishment here. But if you are really bad ... well ... we'll use the paddle."

Henry and Byron looked at each other.

Mr. Kerning walked them back a long hallway lined with rooms, each with two beds. He showed the Kreiser brothers their room—two beds, made perfectly, and two desks with lights. He opened the top drawer and looked them in the eyes to make sure he had their attention. "Top drawer is for underwear and socks." He closed the top and opened the next. "Next down is house clothing. Then play clothes. Hanging in the closet are your school clothes and Sunday best. Never wear play clothes in the house and never wear house clothes outside. Never wear school clothes except when going to school. It's easy. Sunday best only for church."

Henry stepped back, confused. "When do we wear house clothes?"

Mr. Kerning shook his head and sighed. "In the house, Henry. In the house."

The brothers unpacked and then roamed the halls of the home. They sat on the couch behind the others, watching TV. One kid glanced over at them during a commercial. Byron nodded and smiled. Two kids sustained a battle throughout the duration of the evening—throwing pillows tit for tat.

At 9:30, they stopped battling with the pillows when they heard Mrs. Kerning coming down the hall toward the living room. She approached a switch on the wall and flipped it, turning the TV off and a lamp next to it. "Time for bed," she announced.

When Henry went to bed, he pulled the sheet and cover back to get in, but they were tucked tightly and didn't pull back easily. He yanked them, pulling them down into a wad, and then climbed in bed, pulling the wad to cover himself.

In the morning, while it was still dark outside, a bright light came on suddenly, shining on Henry's sleeping face. He woke and saw Byron, disoriented, getting out of bed. Soon their door opened. "Downstairs!" a boy's voice called into their room.

Henry and Byron grabbed some clothes from the

dresser. In the hall, they followed the stream of boys going downstairs. In the changing room they began to change out of their pajamas. The others were all quiet and moved slowly. Henry pulled on his jeans as a black boy approached him.

"Those are play clothes," the boy said.

"Huh?"

"Play clothes."

Henry didn't understand him. He looked at Byron. "What's the black kid saying?"

"You got the wrong clothes, knucklehead," Byron said. Byron looked at the boy and nodded thanks as Henry ran back upstairs.

After getting dressed Byron and Henry got in a line to get a bucket of water from a boy at a big sink. Then another boy in charge of delegating chores sent the brothers off in different directions. Some boys, including the Kreisers, scrubbed Moldavia from the inside while other boys were outside, cleaning windows. After a half hour Byron saw Henry struggle to carry a bucket. Henry rolled his eyes and lifted the bucket to demonstrate that he was in full control. But he wasn't. Water slopped over the edge and splashed on his pants. He dropped the bucket on the floor and even more shot up onto his shirt and splashed his chin.

By the time they finished, the sun had risen and was flooding through the windows on one side of Moldavia, where dormant cornfields stretched off into the distance.

At breakfast Byron and Henry sat across from each other at a long table lined with boys. They watched the morning boy-banter begin. It was noisy, as a volley of jokes bounced from one side of the table to the other. Byron laughed and tried sneak into the conversation while Henry was drawn to two quiet boys at the end of the table. He picked up his plate and went and sat down next to them.

After breakfast, Henry and Byron returned to their room to change into school clothes—slacks and shirts and decent shoes. They stood in front of the mirror and took in their new look—pants came up short, and shirts were tight.

"I can't wear these," Henry said. He began to unbutton his shirt.

"What choice do you have?" Byron asked.

Henry sat on the bed. He shrugged. "I'll wear my clothes."

"No, you won't. Our clothes are 'play clothes' now. Would you just deal with it?"

Outside, they prepared to board the long station wagon with the thirteen other boys.

"There are two kinds of kids at Milton Hershey," one boy said to the Kreisers, as they approached the car. "There are country boys, and there are city boys."

Henry had difficulty deciding which of the five doors to choose. Toward the back he saw mostly white kids. Toward the front there were black and Latin kids. He and Byron squeezed together in a middle seat.

When they pulled up to the school building a few minutes later, the Moldavia station wagon joined a line of dozens of others just like it. The students filed out of the cars, forming a noisy crowd of boys and girls that moved slowly toward the doors of the school building. Henry and Byron milled about with the other Moldavia boys until the bell rang and everyone moved inside quickly. Henry and Byron went to the principal's office as the others went to class.

"Everybody here is assigned a section," the principal said to the brothers. "The section stays together for all classes for the whole school year. I'll write down the location of your first class but then you'll need to follow the others to the next. So on and so forth. Get to know these people."

Henry's first class was full of maps and globes. The other students were already seated when he entered. The teacher was a youngish gentleman with a blue ascot and poof of gray hair that defied his youth. Henry was searching for an empty seat when the teacher nodded. "Welcome to geography, Henry. Everybody, say hi to

Henry." He pointed Henry to take the only open seat in the room, between a girl and a boy.

"Hello, Henry," they all said together as Henry took his seat.

When the class began, a black boy on Henry's left and a blonde-haired girl on his right were whispering to each other, as if Henry wasn't there in between them. Henry tried to pay attention to the teacher, but their conversation was distracting. If he leaned forward, they both leaned back. If he leaned back, they both moved forward.

He followed the group of students after class. He saw Byron walking down the hall with a pack of older boys. In the next class—science—the room was full of animal cages. A warm odor of animals and an undercurrent of disinfectant tickled his nose. A bearded teacher leaned back in his chair as the students assembled; he seemed to be the quiet type. Again, Henry found himself between the black boy and the blonde girl. And again, as the teacher began the lesson, the two whispered around Henry. Annoyed, Henry leaned forward and cupped his ears so he could pay attention the teacher. The boy and girl saw Henry's dismay and quieted themselves.

At the end of the class, the black boy was about to leave but then turned to Henry. "It's not our fault your last name is ..."

"Huh?" Henry said.

"What's your last name?" the boy asked.

"Kreiser."

"It's not our fault your name is Kreiser."

"So? What are you talking about?"

"My last name is King," the boy said. He pointed to the girl. "Her last name is Levy. Before you came, we sat next to each other."

"Oh. Sorry. I can ask to be moved."

The girl laughed. "That's sweet. No reason to ask for anything."

Henry blushed, poked his glasses back on his face, and fiddled with his pencil.

"Donovan King." The boy extended his hand. Henry

shook.

"Sally Levy," the blonde girl said, extending her hand.

Henry looked at her hand and gave it an awkward, shy shake. "Henry Kreiser" he said.

After school, back at Moldavia, Henry was pulled aside by Mr. Kerning. "Come with me, Henry," he said. Henry followed him to a room with lockers. Mr. Kerning pulled a white glove from his jacket pocket. "Did you clean this hobby room, Henry?"

"Yes."

"Yes, *sir*," Mr. Kerning corrected him.

"Huh?"

"You'll respond to me as 'sir.'"

"Okay."

"I repeat, did you clean this room today?" Mr. Kerning pulled the white glove on. He pulled it tight across his hand and wiggled his fingers.

"Yes," Henry responded again.

"Yes, *sir*."

"Oh. Duh. Yes, sir."

"Well, it's not clean."

"It's not?"

Mr. Kerning ran his gloved index finger along the floor. He brought it up to Henry's face. "What do you see?"

"A glove with a speck of dust on it." Henry replied.

"You see the dust?"

"Yeah."

"Yes, *sir*?"

"Yes, sir."

"As you were instructed when you arrived yesterday, disciplinary action is taken when chores aren't completed properly." Mr. Kerning wiggled his fingers out of the glove, taking extra care not to knock the dust off it. "Fifty laps."

Henry looked closely at the glove. "*What?* For that?"

"Don't worry," Mr. Kerning said. "Your brother will be joining you. Apparently, he has trouble listening too. Must be a Kreiser trait."

After dinner, the brothers changed into old running shoes and standard-issue gym shorts. Mr. Kerning walked them outside to the paved circle in front of Moldavia.

Byron ran the circle with great enthusiasm—fast and with agility. Henry stomped along, the school-issued sneakers too heavy for his skinny legs. With each stomp his whole body shook, causing his glasses to creep down his nose in sweat. On each fifth step he poked them back. Byron reached his fifty fast while Henry lost count. When Byron left the circle and walked toward the house, Henry watched but tripped, falling on his face. He pushed himself up without urgency and sat defeated on the asphalt.

Mr. Kerning, who had been watching from the front window, came out of the house, slipping into his jacket. Henry got up immediately and started walking around the circle. Mr. Kerning caught up with Henry but didn't speak. He began walking faster than Henry. Henry laughed and caught up with him. Then Mr. Kerning started jogging. Henry did the same, his feet still stomping. Mr. Kerning lifted his feet high in the air as he jogged, bringing them down softly. His movements were exaggerated for instructive purposes. Henry realized within a few short moments that, by mimicking Kerning's steps, he was able to speed up considerably. Seeing this grown man ahead of him, fully clothed, lifting his feet high in the air, caused Henry to laugh and put a surge in his gait at the same time. He suddenly ran faster and with more strength than he had before. When Mr. Kerning got around the circle, he stopped and leaned on the Moldavia sign. He watched Henry run around the circle several times, and nodded his head each time.

After a dozen more laps, Mr. Kerning held his hand up to stop Henry. "Enthusiasm makes all the difference, doesn't it, young man?"

"Was I going fast?" Henry caught his breath with a proud smile.

Mr. Kerning nodded. "You were." He put a hand on Henry's shoulder. "Let's go in."

During the following week, Henry and Byron took extra care to scrub and wipe every inch of their assigned spaces. One morning Mr. Kerning walked into the recreation room, where Henry was on his hands and knees, scrubbing the floor with a rag. "You're doing a good job, Henry," he said. He gave an approving nod and walked on.

Mrs. Kerning drove the fifteen boys to church on Sunday. All dressed in suits, the pack moved into the church rotunda. From there, they filed into the auditorium. Henry straggled until the pack was about to sit, and then shoved himself in to sit next to Byron.

A robed preacher delivered a nondenominational sermon. It was a simple story told in broad strokes to shine a bright light on a straight path. On the side of the auditorium, boys and girls played handbells. And the student body erupted in song. "Kum bah yah, my lord. Kum bah yah." Henry giggled under his hand then Byron did too. They looked around and watched the hundreds of other boys and girls—some singing with all their hearts, others mechanically moving their lips.

As they left the domed building, the robed preacher stopped them. "You know, there's a Catholic church in town as well."

"Thanks, but we have no way to get there," Byron said.

"Take a bus each Sunday after this service. It waits in the parking lot."

"I don't know. Thank you, but—"

"Come on," the preacher urged. "Continue what your parents started. It's so easy."

"Yes!" Henry exclaimed without hesitation.

"Nah," Byron said.

Henry looked at Byron. "Why won't you?"

"Thanks," Byron said to the preacher. He walked away without answering Henry.

Henry followed Byron. "Why won't you?" he repeated.

"Because of basketball. They play basketball right after this service. Why don't you just go on your own?"

"Should I?" Henry asked.

"If you want."

"Why don't you come too?"

"I just told you," Byron said. "Basketball. Go, Henry!"

Henry ran back to the preacher. "Where do I get the bus?"

* * *

In the coming weeks, Henry spent Sunday afternoons at Saint Gregory's Catholic Church in Hershey town center. And he willingly contributed to the community he found there. He assisted with religion classes after mass, stacking Bibles and taking roll call. One Sunday, Henry took a younger boy aside. The blond boy with glasses was a miniature version of Henry—confused and shy. "God will protect you," Henry told the boy. "You know that, don't you?" And then he saw the boy off to his bus.

The priest watched Henry coming back toward the church a moment later. He laid his hand on Henry's head. "Good work, young man."

Henry looked up at him. "Can I ask you a question Father?"

"Of course."

"How can I become an altar boy?"

The priest took Henry's hands and closed them between the palms of his own. "But do you really want to, Henry?"

"I do."

"We just have to be sure that you are dedicated."

"I am" Henry assured him.

"And you will have to go through training."

"I will."

"Then you will be an altar boy here at St. Gregory's."

In the school hall that week, Henry turned the corner and nearly ran into Sally. "Are you walking over to lunch now?" Henry asked.

"I am but—"

"Come with me," Henry said, warmly.

"Oh. I was waiting for ... I was waiting for ..." She smiled as Donovan approached them.

"Let's walk over to lunch," Donovan said.

"Okay," Sally said.

Henry watched the two of them as they started walking off toward the lunchroom, shoulder to shoulder. Donovan stopped and turned back to Henry. "Let's go."

Sally sat between Donovan and Henry at lunch. She and Donovan chit-chatted endlessly. Henry tried multiple times to get some words in and grew frustrated when he couldn't.

"You're funny, Donovan," Sally laughed as she ate the last spoonful of her fruit cocktail. She dropped the spoon in the bowl. "You really make me laugh."

Henry leaned over her shoulder as she looked at Donovan. "He is funny, isn't he?" Henry said.

"Huh?" She turned to Henry. "Yeah. Yeah. He's funny."

Henry stuck his spoon in his mouth and pushed his ears out. He made a grunting noise and squealed. Donovan laughed. Then Sally turned to Henry and laughed. They all laughed together.

After lunch, they followed the others outdoors into the cool air. Henry ran to a small white birch tree and swung around it, making the yellow leaves fall. Each time he swung around the tree, he made a different funny face for Sally and Donovan. On his fifth time around, on his fifth funny face, Donovan and Sally stopped talking and broke down laughing. They nearly fell over as laughter took their breath away.

"Who are you, Henry Kreiser?" Donovan asked as he gathered himself.

Henry stopped twisting around the tree. "I'm ... I'm ... you said it. Henry Kreiser."

"He knows that, silly," Sally said.

Donovan sat at the base of the tree. Sally and Henry sat down next to him. Henry was in the middle.

"I mean, who *are* you?"

"Do you want to know why I'm here?" Henry asked.

Donovan nodded. "Yeah. You tell your story, and we'll tell ours."

In geography class later that week the teacher stood in

front of a map with a yardstick. "Which is the largest river in the world?" he asked.

Henry raised his hand. "When you say 'largest river,'" he asked, "do you mean the most amount of water or the longest?"

"Good question, Henry," the teacher said. "Which is the largest by water volume, and which is the largest by length?"

"The Amazon. And the Nile," Henry answered. He smiled proudly at Sally and then at Donovan.

After class, they met in the hallway. "Are you that smart in everything?" Donovan asked.

"No, I'm just especially good in geography."

"Really," Sally said. "I'm good in science. And Donovan is good in English. But we both stink at geography."

"I can help you," Henry said as his eyes lit up. "Really, I can help you if you help me with the other classes."

* * *

In the classroom, the budding three-way friendship became a practical arrangement. They each dominated their respective subject, offering help to the other two. Winter came and went. Then spring brought color to the Blue Mountains. The Milton Hershey campus turned green and flowered.

Outside of the classroom, the three-way bond was something more than a practical arrangement. Henry was astonished to see just how fun an amusement park could be with two best friends. At Hershey Park, the rides were packed with screaming kids. Donovan and Sally liked the Super Dooper Looper. Sally and Henry liked the Log Flume. And all three of them liked the Himalaya, a ride they could all fit on together.

In late summer, the park was hot. The three sat on a railing, overlooking the amusements. Sally held a large soda. The waxed paper cup had become soggy with condensation. A white, wooden roller coaster packed with kids sped off, causing all on board to scream. The bell on the whack-a-mole rang and dinged with someone's win.

"Just two more weeks 'til summer's over," Sally said. She passed the soda to Henry.

"Think we'll all be in the same section?" Donovan asked.

Henry slurped the bottom. He jiggled the ice and took off the lid. *I like this place*, he thought. "I sure hope we're all in the same section," he said.

After church the next week, Donovan and Sally approached Henry in the parking lot. "We're gonna meet at the park this afternoon. Near the Comet," Sally said.

"Come with us." Donovan threw his arm across Henry's shoulder.

"Aw man," Henry said. "I can't. I have to go to church."

"Why you gonna do that?" Donovan asked. "Only one more week left for the park, and you're gonna go sit through another hour of church?"

"Yeah. I'm assisting in religion classes for the little ones, so I really can't skip it."

"Dang." Donovan shook his head in regret. "Well, next week is the last week. Let's be sure we all go on Saturday."

While riding home from church on the bus that day, still wearing his Sunday best, Henry peered into Hershey Park through the vines on the fence. As if by destiny, he spotted Sally and Donovan running into the gates of the log flume. He saw Sally push Donovan playfully.

Back at Moldavia, Byron walked in the bedroom as Henry was taking off his suit. Byron was dripping with sweat and had a basketball in his hands.

"Don't forget," Byron said as he fell back on his bed. "We're going home next weekend."

"What?"

"Kate is taking us home for the weekend."

"But ... I have to stay here!" Henry declared.

"For what?" Byron asked.

"I just have to... we don't need to go home, do we?"

"She wants to see us."

Henry folded his tie and put it into the drawer. He

shrugged.

"You don't want to see Kate and the others?" Byron asked. "Maybe we'll see Dad, too."

After a moment, Henry nodded. "Yeah, I do. Of course I do."

When Henry and Byron arrived back in Levittown, they found that Kate and Jack had bought a small home. It was in a section of Levittown where the homes were a bit smaller than the one they grew up in. Theirs was a pleasant green house with asbestos siding, among others in blues and yellows. Dinner was on the table before long—beef stroganoff, broccoli with Cheez Whiz, stuffed potatoes, and Wonder Bread with butter.

"Are we going to see Dad?" Henry asked.

"He's coming tomorrow," Kate said. "Okay?"

"Yeah."

Henry watched the front drive through the kitchen window the next morning. A mystery man on a motorcycle arrived and sat in front of the house. His helmet stayed on his head, but Henry could see a beard. He watched the man smoke cigarettes, one after the next, until finally; Kate went out to talk to him. Then, as the helmet came off, Henry connected the dots and recognized the man—it was Dad.

"Dad!" Henry ran out, followed by Byron. They hugged and smiled and patted Dad on the back. Henry ogled the bike—a cruiser with a wide black seat and sissy bar for a passenger. Henry went to touch the chrome muffler but Kate grabbed his hand to stop him. "Its hot!" she warned.

"Take me for a ride," he said to Dad.

"No," Kate said. "Motorcycles are dangerous."

"Get on," Dad said.

Henry jumped on as Kate shook her head.

"We'll be back for you, young man," Dad said to Byron. He put the helmet on Henry's head.

Henry wrapped his arms around Dad's waist and held on tightly. Dad's leather jacket smelled of cigarettes and motor oil. They rode through suburbs, on highways, and on quiet streets. When they stopped at a traffic light Henry leaned forward. "Where do you live now, Dad?" he asked.

Dad didn't answer.

"Will you stay with us tonight?" Henry asked a few minutes later.

"I'll stay."

They rode through some hills and passed a lake. At a golf course, Dad stopped the motorcycle. They got off, and Dad pulled a brown paper bag from under the seat. "See that tree?" Dad asked, pointing to a wide old tree in the middle of the golf course.

"Yeah?"

"That's the means to our survival."

Henry stared at the tree. "What do you mean?"

"Nourishment," Dad said. "It grows and produces fruit for our nourishment." He started off toward the tree. Henry paused for a moment then followed.

"What are we doing here?" Henry asked as a golf cart passed nearby.

"I already told you Henry." When Dad climbed the tree to shake the branches, Henry stood below. He caught some pears, while others hit the ground. One fell and knocked him on the head. After stuffing dozens of them in the brown paper bag, Henry and Dad and each ate a pear. When two golfers rode by in a cart, Henry saw one stare. He took another bite and stared back.

"Dad?" he asked.

"Yes." Dad was looking off in the distance as he scavenged every ounce of flesh from the pear with his front teeth.

"Do you go to church?"

Dad tucked the pear core under a leaf. He turned his attention to Henry. "Of course I don't."

"Why?" Henry asked.

"Don't ask me that question."

"Why not?"

"Because, your mom asked me to go every week. I never went and never will because I don't believe."

"But why don't you believe?"

"The question is: why *do* you believe?"

Henry stood and threw the core of his pear at a flag on the green. The golfers watched and shook their heads.

"I asked you a question," Dad said. "Why do *you* believe?"

Henry shrugged. "Because God made us."

"He made us? Are you sure?"

"Yes. It says so in the Bible," Henry said, proud of the statement.

"Did you learn about evolution yet?"

"What?"

"Evolution. That's what made us," Dad corrected Henry.

"So evolution is something God made, then?"

"No, Henry. Evolution was made by nature. It proves God doesn't exist. We made God."

"Ha! How did we make God? We're not that powerful."

"With our imaginations. We are primates." Dad held up his thumb. "We only grew smart because of our thumbs. And we developed consciousness. We got too curious for our own good and painted ourselves into a corner. That's when we created God to ease our curiosity."

Henry walked around to the far side of the tree, barely listening to Dad. He slowly returned, kicking leaves, and grabbed another pear from the bag. He fiddled with it in his hand. "What does that have to do with God?"

"Religion is just a way to govern people. Jesus Christ, Henry ..."

"What?"

"I said, Jesus Christ, who you know about, was not necessarily the son of God. He was just a smart guy in the right place at the right time with good ideas about how to help people get along."

"Huh?" Henry tossed the pear in the air. "So you don't believe in God, but you believe in Jesus Christ?"

"I believe he was a man. A smart man, like you will be some day."

Henry held the pear out in one hand. He tried to process all that Dad had just told him, but it just added up to rambling nonsense. He pressed his thumb into the pear. "I believe in God."

"How old are you now?"

"Twelve."

"Someday you'll understand." Dad approached Henry, put his hand on his shoulder and reached to take the pear from his hand. "You'll understand to believe only in what you see and feel—like the nourishment this tree just provided you."

"No." Henry held the pear from Dad and squeezed it harder.

"You will."

"No!" The pear broke apart in Henry's hand.

"Why'd you do that?" Dad asked. "We're going to eat these pears."

"Because you said you were going to try to bring us back together again, and we're still not together."

Dad grew silent and picked up the bag of pears. They walked back across the golf course to the motorcycle.

"You have to understand, Henry, my plans change as I learn more and more about what I have to do," Dad said as he packed the bag of pears on the motorcycle. "I'm certain one day you will understand but I realize now it might be difficult for you."

"What do you have to do?"

"I'm not sure yet. But I know I'm figuring it out."

As they passed through the next town, a police car followed behind them. Dad watched in his rearview mirror as he turned slowly into the A&P grocery.

"Damn it," Dad said. Henry saw flashing lights in the rearview mirror. He turned and saw the police car had pulled in behind them.

"No helmet today, sir?" the officer asked as he approached the motorcycle.

Dad shook his head as he got off the motorcycle. "As you can see, I'm letting my son wear the helmet."

"I see. Whose bike is it?" the officer asked as he walked around the bike. "No license plate?"

Dad stepped up to the officer and took him by the arm. "I needed to see my son," he said, moving into the officer's comfort zone. "I'm sure you understand."

The officer stepped backwards and pulled Dad's hand off of him in one movement. "Sorry, sir. The law doesn't allow us to make exceptions. We're going to have to impound your bike."

"Do you realize by taking the motorcycle you are reducing our ability to move freely?" Dad asked the officer.

The officer looked in Dad's eyes and saw unblinking seriousness. He didn't know how to respond. "You can retrieve the motorcycle at the station on Main Street," he told Dad. "You'll need to pay a ticket and show registration and insurance."

A truck soon arrived to take the motorcycle.

Dad and Henry had no way to get back to Kate's with their bag of pears so the police took them in the patrol car.

That evening, back at Kate's house, Dad set up camp out back. In a Crock-Pot plugged in between a hedge and a garden hose, he prepared the pears. Henry, Byron, and Kate came out after dinner. They sat on the grass with Dad and ate warm pear sauce as they looked across the backyards of the other homes.

Near midnight, Henry got out of bed and looked out the living room window. Dad had set up a lean-to with a blue tarp and a flash light glowed underneath of it.

In the morning, Dad was ready to move on. Kate lent him her bicycle and Dad methodically strapped on all of his possessions. After a quick hug Henry and Byron watched him ride away, struggling to control the bike with all the weight on it, until he turned the corner down the road. Then they sat on the lawn.

Kate came out and sat down with them. "Dad is brilliant. You know that?" she said.

"He seems lost," Byron said. "Why doesn't he have a car?"

"Well sometimes intelligence leads to crazy ideas. And those ideas make people do crazy things. He doesn't believe in owning a car."

"That doesn't make sense." Henry was still staring down the road where Dad disappeared around the corner.

Kate tapped Henry's shoulder to get him to turn and face her. "He'll come around." She put her arms around them. "We're his children. He'll do what he needs to do to make our lives right."

They went to church with Kate that morning. Henry praised God vigorously; stood up, sat down. He clenched the hymn book, always opened to the right page, and sang from deep inside his chest. During a moment of silence, he prayed: *Dear Lord, please help my dad. Help him stay alive. Help him see the light of your love. Amen.*

The following Saturday, back at school, Henry took a skateboard and went off the Moldavia property. He found the steepest hill, across the field and up the road, and then rode it down. Gravity pulled him down around the curve until another slope going upward eventually brought the board to a stop. He sat down on the skateboard in front of a student home with a massive front lawn. Along the side of the house with the carport, several girls were playing basketball. Henry watched. A girl dressed in white played especially well—a blonde girl. When she took the ball for an outside shot, Henry recognized her movements and looked closely. It was Sally. He got off his board quickly to leave but then froze and watched her. Her hair was pulled back and tied; her shorts and shirt clung with perspiration. She dribbled. A girl lunged at her. She dropped back and shot. The defending girl swung and missed. All screamed. The ball hit the rim and shot off. It bounced down the driveway and rolled toward the road. Henry's heart fired double-time when Sally darted after it. Seeing the ball coming, he turned to leave but was too late—she had seen him, and the ball was at his feet.

"Henry? What are you doing down here?"

"I ... was ... I was riding my skateboard." He pointed up the hill. He reached down and grabbed the ball. He fumbled with it. He poked his glasses back on his nose. She put out her hands to receive the ball. He threw it, but it went over her head, bounced on the driveway, and fell into the grass.

She laughed. "Nice throw, Kreiser." She chased after the ball, grabbed it, and ran back up the driveway.

Henry watched her as she dribbled away. He watched her hair braid flop on her white, wet shirt. When she stopped running and got ready to shoot, he watched the braid fall to rest between her shoulders. *Nice throw, Kreiser*, he thought. *Nice throw, Kreiser. Nice, stupid, stupid throw, Kreiser.* He picked up the skateboard and walked up the hill.

At summer's end Byron packed his belongings in boxes as Henry sat on the bed watching.

"I don't understand why you can't just stay here," Henry said. "Or why I can't go up to Senior Division with you."

"Is that what's been bothering you?"

Henry shrugged.

"Well. They have to have rules. They just can't let anybody go anywhere. And Senior Division is across town. How would you get to school?"

"I could ride a bike."

"You don't have a bike, and they don't allow bikes here."

"They should."

"Listen, Henry! It doesn't matter if they *should*. They *don't*."

Henry grew quiet.

"Okay?" Byron asked.

"You don't have to yell."

"Well, you know... I don't like for us to be separated either."

"It bothers you, too?" Henry asked.

"Of course. I think it's stupid."

After a long spell of quiet, Byron reached into the cardboard box he was packing and pulled out a little boom box. "Do you want my boom box? You can have it."

"Really?"

"Yeah. I'm getting a new one."

"Thanks." Henry pushed and turned the buttons and knobs on the boom box as Byron finished packing.

CHAPTER 4

It was the first day of the new school year. Boys and girls read from mimeographed papers on a bulletin board in the hallway. Among the crowd that pushed forward were Sally and Donovan. Henry, too, pushed to the front to find his name and section assignment.

"Seven-six," Henry said.

"Seven-six," Sally turned to Donovan.

"Aw, man." Donovan put his arms over both of their shoulders.

"What section?" Henry asked as Sally waited for the answer.

"Seven-three," Donovan said.

"Seven-*three*?" Sally became flustered.

"It's just me and you, Sally," Henry said, nudging her with a smile.

She ran off.

"Sally! We'll see each other at lunch each day!" Donovan called. "It's cool."

In their new science classroom, where planets and diagrams filled the walls, Henry and Sally sat side by side. Sally rested her chin in her hands as the teacher paced back and forth, giving highlights of the coming semester. The new teacher was tall and lanky and wore a tweed jacket with sleeves too short. Moving on to the day's lesson the teacher held up an ant farm. "What's behind the glass?"

Henry stood. "Thousands of ants?"

"Very good, Kreiser." He looked out over the class.

"These ants work. They work day in and day out. Do you know why?"

Nobody raised a hand.

"They work to serve their queen. They exist to serve their queen. Now, we're going to watch a video." He pulled a screen down in front of the blackboard. He turned down the lights. "This is a movie of a colony of ants that have lost the scent of their queen." In the back of the room, he turned on a projector.

On the screen, hundreds of thousands of ants walked along in a thick column. Suddenly, they ceased to move, backed up en masse and began moving again. The back and forth motion continued and slowly the column bent as some moved in one direction while more moved in other directions. After several minutes, the column bent so much that it formed a circle and the inner part of the circle bunched up, transforming the mass of ants into an increasingly fast-moving vortex. Frantic ants climbed over slower ones until they were all scrambling, and the mass spun while inching along in no particular direction. Henry was amazed.

The teacher turned the projector off. "In the absence of their queen, their leader, they will all die."

Henry stared speechless at the blank screen. When the lights were back on, he looked over at Sally. She still sat with her chin on her hands.

"An ant colony is considered a super-organism," the teacher continued. "A super-organism is defined as a collection of organisms in which labor is highly specialized and where individuals are not able to survive by themselves for extended periods of time."

Henry raised his hand. "But what happens when they ..."

"Yes, Kreiser?"

"But what happens when the ants move ... from where ... why are they doing that?"

"As I said, because they lost the scent of the queen."

When the bell rang, Henry approached the teacher. "I still don't understand why the ants did that," he said.

"They lost the scent of the queen. They exist only for the queen."

Henry nodded and thought about it. "It still doesn't make sense to me."

The teacher got up. "I like your curiosity Henry. When I was your age I was the same way. I have an idea." The teacher reached into the desk drawer and pulled out a book. He handed it to Henry. "This may help."

Henry turned it in his hand. "*The Origin of Species*."

"You are a little young for this, but since you asked ... It's about evolution."

Over the next week, Henry read the book cover to cover. He understood very little. But he clung to every word. He felt the book's authority and more importantly, its loyalty to truth. That was enough to send a shiver down his spine. In the September cool nights most kids at Moldavia slept soundly, but Henry tossed and turned.

The following Sunday after Catholic church, the priest saw Henry sitting idle in a pew, seemingly deep in thought. The priest approached him. "Are you ready to start altar-boy training?" the priest asked.

"Hmm. Maybe in a couple of weeks. I have to get permission to stay in the afternoons." Henry paused. "But I have another question."

"Shoot, young man." The priest sat down and put his arm over Henry's shoulder.

"If Adam and Eve were the first humans," Henry said, "and they were created by God, when did evolution happen?"

"Well, Henry. That's a big question. There's no easy answer except to say that evolution is just a theory. You have to believe with your heart. God speaks to your heart every Sunday. Does he not?"

"Yeah."

"And hasn't he told you that Adam and Eve were created by him?"

"Yes."

"And has he ever mentioned evolution? Do you see any proof of that in the Bible?"

"No. But it's true. I just read *The Origin of Species*."

"Oh." The priest nodded his head. "I see. Well, as I said, evolution is just a theory. And you should also know that faith is important."

"What do you mean, faith is important?"

"I mean some things just don't need to be questioned. You have to have faith in the word of the Lord."

That week, in science class, Henry stood next to his desk, shortly after answering one of the teacher's questions.

"Yes, Kreiser. Absolutely right."

Henry sat down with a big smile. He looked at Sally as the bell rang.

"Test next week!" the teacher announced as the students began filing out the door.

Sally shook her head. "If you didn't raise your hand so fast, I could have answered that question."

"But I knew it first."

"No, you raised your hand first," she huffed. "You should give other people a chance."

Henry shrugged. "Sorry. But listen, I've been meaning to ask you ..."

She grabbed her books and got up. "What, Henry?"

"Do you want to go ..."

"What?"

"Ah, forget it. Forget it."

On Sunday, after the Milton Hershey School church service, dozens of kids broke away to approach the buses for secondary worship service. Henry approached the one with the sign reading "Saint Gregory's Catholic Church." He stepped up one step, hesitated for a moment, then turned and got off.

"Where you going, Kreiser?" a boy yelled from the bus.

"Can't go this week!"

Henry found the Moldavia station wagon before it pulled away. As he climbed in, Mrs. Kerning saw him in the rearview mirror. "No church today? No religion classes?"

"I have to study for a big test tomorrow."

That evening after dinner Henry stayed at his desk with his nose in his science text book.

When he sat down to take the test the next day he felt confident he knew all the answers and finished quickly.

In science class a few days later, the teacher stood at the front of the room and announced, "Tests have been scored. Henry Kreiser. Please step forward."

Henry stepped up.

"This young man," Teacher said, "got all the questions right, as well as the extra credit. One hundred ten percent."

When Henry sat down, he looked over at Sally's paper. It had ninety-five percent written at the top. She saw him look at her paper, so she put her hand over her score.

After class, Henry approached the teacher.

"Yes, Henry, how may I help you?"

"I was thinking maybe I could help out here... in class."

"You mean to be an assistant?"

"Yeah. Like that. An assistant."

"It's a lot of extra work. Are you sure you want it?"

"Definitely." Henry squeezed the text book in his hand and nodded proudly.

* * *

Science class became a new outlet for Henry's passion. In his role as assistant, he collected and collated papers, and during tests he stood vigilantly to watch for cheats. On lab days, he laid out instructions and supplies.

At the end of class one day, the teacher put his hand on Henry's head as the others filed out. "Maybe someday you'll be a science teacher."

Henry was about to respond, but then he saw Sally coming toward him. He waited until she was within earshot and turned back to the teacher. "I will. But first I'll be a scientist. And I'll work with the animals out in the wild. I'll lead research teams and collect information."

Henry took a proud, deep breath. "I'll make discoveries that will make the world a better place."

Sally rolled her eyes and left the room.

That year, Henry's physicality changed. He experienced a growth spurt, which made him appear skinnier. Pimples flourished in his face. His eyesight grew worse, and he had to get thicker glasses.

While walking in the hall one day, he passed a group of older boys. They turned to watch as Henry walked by. One of them coughed loudly, and Henry thought he heard something under the cough. Then another one of them coughed, and Henry knew immediately that the boys were saying something – a single word that they were concealing under their coughs. When the third boy coughed, Henry finally understood the word: "nerd."

Henry stopped going to the Catholic church and threw himself into science. It was isolating and lonely, but he relished the social silence and cherished the acquisition of knowledge. The seed planted by *The Origin of Species* flourished into an ecosystem of scientific facts that rationally made little sense but brought him peace of mind.

In a mid-October science class, as the boys and girls took their seats, one of the boys who called Henry a nerd a few weeks earlier now approached him.

"Kreiser, can I ask you a question about the homework?"

Henry didn't answer or even look the boy in the face. He just turned over the paper on his desk to conceal his work.

The teacher pulled down the screen. "So ... primates, including humans, are highly social. Their well-being, their social status, and therefore the likelihood they will pass on their genes is highly dependent on their ability to socialize."

As the teacher moved to the projector in the back, Henry shot his hand up. "Henry?"

"Right. But when humans developed thumbs they became different."

"Yes. Well, it's not exactly like that." The teacher turned down the lights.

"Yes, it is," Henry insisted. "They developed thumbs and then got bigger brains, which means they acted differently."

"No, Henry. That's only partially right. But it's off topic anyway. We'll discuss how evolution gave rise to these things later in the year."

"Yeah. But that's how we—"

"Henry! May I play the movie?!"

Everybody looked at Henry. He blushed from the sudden attention. He looked at Sally, who stared at him in disbelief for a second then turned away, embarrassed for him.

On the screen the jungle came alive. Gorillas picked and preened each other. Then, in a battle, they beat on their chests. Behind a tree, two adults moved in unison. Their pelvic movements led to grunts. The kids in class laughed. Henry, still reeling from the teacher's reproach and Sally's scorn, shifted in his chair, turned to the side, and looked at Sally's side—at the area where her waist curved inward. Then more gorilla grunts. Henry grew angry and wanted Sally to commiserate with him, but she ignored him now. The film's British narrator explained the gorillas' sexual intercourse with the most clinical words possible. Henry saw Sally's shirt buttons straining under puberty's growing influence. She shifted back in her seat and put her hands in her lap. He looked at where her hands had fallen and watched her slide them between her thighs to cozy up for the movie. Henry gasped. He looked at the screen, and then back at her, and then back at the screen again.

In his bedroom that evening, Henry pulled out the boom box for the first time since Byron left it. Switching through the stations he found a pop song that started in a melancholic key—a synthesized melody, drums, and snares. Madonna vocals started sensually. "Borderline" was the song. Henry's eyes glazed. Madonna sang the song about wanting and understanding and love. He lay back on the bed, and his hand flip-flopped over to his lap.

He searched for his zipper and imagined Sally in science class. He opened his pants. He showed her diagrams to show her how. She evaded and he followed. They stopped in the back, behind the projector, and the lights went out. The movie clicked and clacked with the sounds of gorilla love. Henry laid her down. Suddenly, his bed was there behind the projector. Henry slid his hand in her pants and it slipped and slid in wisps of hair. Sexy vocals coaxed him on. "Borderline" kept him on—soothed him—aroused him into a frenzy. Dizzy frenzy made his hand move fast. Pop song pleasure made climax quick. Slight loss of consciousness, then utter shock.

He pulled his hand away quickly and lay there frozen, looking at the mess on his belly. Then, when somebody knocked on the door, he got up quickly. And in one adept movement, he grabbed a sock and wiped, zipped, and tucked.

"I'm busy!" he yelled.

* * *

In the coming months, Henry came again and again to that nexus in his imagination. While he floundered socially in the real world, especially with respect to Sally, he was master of the universe in his imagined world—a world of science diagrams and melancholy pop songs. Not coincidentally, he became more hunched, as if his posture was adapting to his lifestyle of reading textbooks and masturbating.

Mr. Kerning asked Henry into Moldavia's office one day. The paddle still hung there on the wall.

"What did I do wrong?" Henry asked as he sat down in front of the desk.

"Nothing at all. You've been good—really good. But I'm concerned about you."

Henry looked at his right hand. "Why?"

"When boys grow quiet at your age we need to ask why."

Henry shrugged. Mr. Kerning stared at him.

"You know you can tell me anything you like." Mr. Kerning got up from his chair. He stood next to Henry and put his hand on his shoulder. "Let's go fishing this Saturday. How about that?"

Mr. Kerning and Henry waded into the Susquehanna River, both wearing waist-high wader boots. The river was shallow there, and rapids ran fast through. On the far bank, the trees had turned to golden browns and reds and yellows. A rocky cliff gave a far drop for falling leaves. Henry fumbled at first with the rod and reel. Mr. Kerning moved his hands slowly for instructional purposes—pulled the line out near the reel, held the rod behind himself, slung the rod, and let the line go. Henry watched each time and tried again. He slapped himself with the hook and sinker. The worm fell off and stuck to his sleeve. Then, finally, he got it. He cast far with ease.

For hours they cast. They let the worm sit in the water and then reeled it in. Then one time, while reeling in, Henry screamed, "I got one!" He yanked at the rod.

"Hold still," Kerning said. "Hold the rod still for a second."

Henry continued to yell and yank. And then his glasses fell off his face. "My glasses!" In one movement he dropped the rod and fell forward and plunged into water. Mr. Kerning leaped over, grabbed Henry by the straps on his waders, and pulled him up out of the water. Henry gasped for air as he sputtered the water from his mouth. In his hand were his glasses.

"Where's the rod?" Mr. Kerning asked.

Henry shrugged. He put on his glasses.

"Well, find the rod, please."

Henry hesitated, looking down into the water. "Maybe the fish took it."

"You didn't have a fish."

"Yes, I did. I felt it."

"No, you had a snag. The hook was stuck in a rock. Can you try to find the rod?"

Henry looked in the water again, but then his glasses began sliding down his face. He held them in place and looked at Mr. Kerning.

"Go into shore," Mr. Kerning said. "Here—take my rod. I'll find yours."

"I had a fish. I swear."

"No, you didn't. There are no fish in the river at this time of year."

"No fish? Then why are we fishing?"

"Because... we're practicing for when the fish come back next spring."

Henry shivered on the river bank as Mr. Kerning searched for and found the rod.

That week, Donovan, Sally and Henry sat together in the lunchroom. Their conversation was particularly dull. Sally had finished eating and was watching Donovan finish. Henry looked over occasionally from his bowl of chocolate pudding.

"How are classes?" Donovan asked. "You both doing well?"

"They're great," Henry said.

"It's all right," Sally said. "Not the same without you."

"Yeah," Henry said, "definitely not the same."

"I sit next to the twins now," Donovan said. "They are *so* cute."

Sally went back to her empty pudding bowl. She scraped it with her spoon. "You think they're cute? I think they have weird faces—like their noses seem crooked or something."

"Why would you say that?" Donovan asked. "I'm going steady with Heather."

Sally dropped her spoon in her bowl. "Oh, I'm sorry. You're goin' out with her?!"

"Yeah, we've been seeing..." Donovan started. "Yeah, we're goin' steady."

Henry slapped Donovan on the back. "That's awesome!"

"I gotta go." Sally stood and grabbed her tray. "You guys are so immature." She walked away.

"Whoa. What's wrong with her?" Donovan asked.

"Who knows?" Henry shrugged.

On Henry's thirteenth birthday, Kate took him and Byron back to Levittown for the weekend. Henry watched out the car window on the drive. December cold meant leafless trees. When they turned down a road Henry didn't recognize, he leaned forward. "Wait," he said. "Where are we going? I thought we were going to Dad's."

She didn't respond.

"What's going on?" Byron asked.

Kate stared straight ahead at the road. "I've been meaning to tell you ... Dad's not well."

"What do you mean?" Byron asked. He looked back to see if Henry was listening. "You want to tell me later?"

"Tell us now." Henry leaned forward.

"He's not in the apartment anymore," she said. She tilted the rearview mirror so she could see Henry's face. "He's on the street."

"Homeless?" Byron asked as Henry looked out the window.

"I wouldn't say that. He's living in a truck—the old ice cream truck from Mr. Watson."

Kate pulled into an Exxon service station on Pine Street in Langhorne, across from the shopping center with a Shop-n-Bag, a Laundromat, and a Hallmark store. They parked in a gravel lot. In front of them was an old ice cream truck up on blocks. On the side of the truck, paintings of creamy treats were long worn thin and cracked away.

"He lives *there*?" Henry asked.

Kate nodded. "He does. I'll stay in the car."

"I'll go in after you," Byron told Henry.

As Henry approached the truck, Dad pushed open the metal door on the back of the truck. His beard was long now and disheveled. He was thin as a rail and Henry barely recognized him.

Happy Birthday, Henry. Come into my home."

Inside the truck was tight and simple—mat, bike, and propane stove. On a shelf above were some bottles. Stacks of papers sat on a wheel well that served as a desk. Some pens and pencils lay on a notepad with a page half-written. Dad closed the notepad. "I'm surviving here. Cold. But at night I just go down into the ground and let my body and fur keep me warm." He reached toward the stack of papers and pulled out a piece of cardboard. A striking wilderness photo was affixed to it—rugged mountains, a lake, a meadow. On the photo were two hand-painted animals, an eagle in red and a horse in yellow. He handed it to Henry. Henry touched the eagle and turned the card over in his hands. Some words were written on the back in pencil. Hand-drawn lines kept the letters in line.

> Happy Birthday, Henry
> A wise man once said:
> The more birthdays the better.
> He meant, something new
> is a birthday to you, so every
> day could be for you, when you
> stay young.
> Love,
> Dad

Henry stared at it for a long moment. "Thanks, Dad."

"Well, happy birthday."

Henry sat quietly. He looked around.

"Do you know what the card means?" Dad asked.

Henry looked at it again. "Uh ... it means to stay young."

"Yeah, kind of. The eagle and the horse on the front represent freedom to live."

"Freedom to live?"

"Yeah. And freedom to be whoever you want to be."

"Thanks."

"Who do you want to be, Henry?"

Henry looked through the front window of the ice

cream truck to the Shop-n-Bag, where people went in and out with their groceries. He saw a woman park a station wagon and go in the grocery store with her young son.

"I want to be a scientist, Dad." Henry looked at Dad proudly. "I stopped going to church."

Dad nodded. He shuffled through some of his papers.

"Did you hear me? I want to be a scientist. I'm done with church."

"I heard you."

Henry waited for a response.

Dad shuffled some more and then put the papers down. "That concerns me—that you want to give your life to science."

"Why?"

"You see these papers here, Henry?" Dad poked the stack. "In here, I explain why science should not be trusted."

"What do you mean?"

"Don't you know how it all started? Don't you know what they say?"

"Yes. I do. I'm not stupid," Henry argued. "Evolution."

"No. Before that."

"Yes. I know that too. The big bang."

"No, after the big bang. How did life start?"

Henry thought about it for a moment then shrugged his shoulders.

"That's because nobody knows. They have some theory of lightning zapping the primordial soup. But that's all they have."

"Okay, fine. So, that's what I'm going to figure out."

Dad grabbed his arm. "No!" Henry gasped with fear. Dad released his arm. "What you don't understand is that science is as bad as religion. It's worse than religion."

"I don't know what you're talking about."

"Well listen then. Science is weapon, and you should stay away from it. They used it against me. That's why I'm living in this truck. Because they wanted to expel me from society, and they used science to do that." He grabbed his papers. "That's what this is all about! That's why I'm going to dispel science all together. The very foundation of it is meaningless. They use it to create medicines so they can control our minds and keep us behaving how they want us to. It's all poison!"

Henry didn't know how to respond. Dad pulled his notepad out and wrote a few lines.

"Dad?"

Dad continued to write.

"Dad!"

"Yes, Henry?"

"When are you going to get our house back so we can all live together again?"

"I'm going to die, Henry. And I need to finish my work before that happens."

"Maybe you're not. They said that five years ago."

"No. I am. Soon."

Henry stood up. He looked through the newspapers on the shelf. "Maybe you should try to get better. If we lived in a house, maybe you would be better."

"Better? You think there's something wrong with me too?"

"No. I didn't mean that—"

"Give it up, Henry. Go on with your life!"

Henry stood still for a moment, unable to process the aggression, then ran out the metal door and jumped down to the ground. He stood outside of the truck, breathing heavily, as if he was going to cry. But then he shook it off and went back to the car.

* * *

April showers pounded Hershey for days. At lunch one day, the students, unable to go outside, congregated in groups in the hallways. Boom boxes lined the long main hall of the school. Heavy metal music could be heard outside of the wood shop. Rap music was played near the gymnasium. And in the small English and Foreign Language wing, a dozen kids gathered around a boom box playing pop music.

Sally and Donovan were sitting on the carpet nearby as a Duran Duran song played. On his way back from the bathroom Henry heard Sally speaking to Donovan in a hushed tone.

"There's something I need to tell you before Henry gets back," she said.

Henry stopped a few feet away, out of sight behind a bulletin board.

"Okay," Donovan said.

"I think he likes me."

"Yeah. We're all good friends. Right?"

"No. I think he *likes* me."

"Oh. Nah. Maybe you misinterpreted something."

Henry walked out into their view.

"No Donovan. It's obvious. But more importantly, I like ..." She paused when she saw Henry coming.

"You like?"

"I ... oh, nothing."

Henry sat down next to Sally. No one spoke as they watched others dance around to Duran Duran. Henry started to say something to Sally several times but then stopped before uttering a word.

Another song soon started with triumphant notes, then quieted down. Paul McCartney's voice sang "Ebony and Ivory." He sang to the Lord about people, black and white, living in harmony.

Sally got up and walked away, without saying anything to them.

They both watched her turn at the end of the hallway.

"I think she likes me," Henry said. "She gets all flustered when I'm around." Henry got up and grabbed an invisible microphone. He started swaying and looked at Donovan. When the Paul McCartney vocals started again, he lip-synched along. Donovan, reluctant at first, grabbed his own invisible microphone and lip-synched the opposing lyrics with Stevie Wonder.

But then the boy at the boom box hit stop suddenly and the group burst out in laughter.

Donovan walked off.

AMERICAN SPAZ

"Donovan!" Henry chased after him.

Donovan stopped. "They think you're a dork!"

"What?"

"You saw how they were laughing."

"I don't care. And Sally doesn't care either."

"Who?"

"I like Sally" Henry declared. "I really like Sally."

"Well, you gotta wake up and stop that, too."

"Why? No. I'm not gonna stop liking her."

"Henry! When are you going to realize she doesn't like you?"

Henry had no response. He walked over to the wall and sat on the floor. Donovan followed and sat next to Henry.

"It's not your fault, man," Donovan said. "You're a nice guy. But she likes the more athletic type. She likes black kids and you're the whitest guy I know."

Henry shook his head. "No. She'll like me. I know what she likes. She's smart and I'm smart. That's why we'll make a good couple. She just doesn't know I like her, so she's pretending she doesn't like me." Henry got up and left Donovan sitting there against the wall.

Back at Moldavia, in the living room, Mr. Kerning stood in front of Henry wearing the white glove. "Did you clean this room?"

"Yeah."

"Yes, sir?"

"Yes, sir."

He ran the white glove along the floor board. He brought it up to Henry's face. "What do you see?"

"A speck of dust."

"A speck? How about a clump?"

Henry shrugged.

"Fifty laps."

Henry ran a few laps and then got tired so he started walking. Mr. Kerning slipped on his jacket and went outside. He caught up with Henry and began walking faster, trying to inspire him to do the same. But Henry didn't respond. He continued walking slowly, staring off into another place. Mr. Kerning came around again and passed Henry, garnering no attention. Then he stopped and leaned on the Moldavia sign. He watched Henry walk by once. And then on the second time Mr. Kerning sighed and shook his head. "One hundred laps," he said to Henry. He went in as Henry continued walking his laps.

In the carport Mrs. Kerning was watching a few of the boys sweep debris into a corner. Mr. Kerning joined her. "I feel like we're losing Henry," he confided in her.

The following day in science class, the teacher spoke about the beginning of the universe. Henry paid little attention, as he was glancing often at Sally. His glasses were on his desk. He scribbled a picture of two hearts intertwined. One time, when he glanced over, Sally gave him an unfriendly glance, annoyed that he was looking over so much. With his blurry vision, though, Henry misread her look. He sensed she was conveying desire for him. He folded the picture of the two hearts and passed it to her. She opened it and couldn't believe her eyes. She crumpled it and set it aside. Henry stared at the crumpled paper, and a dark side of him rose inside. He heard the boy behind Sally giggle.

Henry put on his glasses and shot the boy a dirty look.

"Is there a problem?" the teacher asked.

Silence.

"Kreiser, something to add about the big bang? The early beginnings of planet Earth?"

Henry shrugged.

"You were the star of this class," the teacher stood. "But you haven't added anything in quite some time."

Henry sat up straight.

The teacher sighed. "Tonight's assignment," he said to the class, "a two-page essay on any subject we covered this year."

That night Henry sat at his desk, thinking about what to write for his essay. He thought about evolution. He thought about Sally. He thought about the big bang. Then he tried to think about the big bang and evolution together. *When did evolution start?* he thought. *When did it all start?* He opened his textbook and found the chapter on evolution and read page after page. In a little blue box, the "Oparin-Haldane scenario" was explained. It described the beginning. Lightning zapped primordial soup and suddenly life began. Bacteria formed and natural selection took place. Hundreds of billions of years later, there were humans. Henry turned the page to find a new chapter. He turned to the paper and wrote furiously.

In science class the next day, the students all sat with their papers in front of them.

The teacher pointed to Henry. "Kreiser, come forward and read your essay."

Henry stepped to the front of the class. He cleared his throat. "I chose to write about the moment that life started. It was the very second that the primordial soup gave birth to the first self-replicating bacteria. According to the Oparin-Haldane scenario, this happened as a result of lightning zapping through the primordial soup. But I don't believe it."

A couple of kids in class chuckled. Henry continued. "This is an example of how science, like religion, is made up by people. And if I don't believe that theory, then I must not believe evolution—another theory. Or anything else. Right? So I choose to not make this essay two pages since I've made my point in two paragraphs."

A few kids erupted in laughter. Others looked at each other in disbelief. Henry looked at Sally smugly. She shook her head in dismay. Barely audible, Henry said, "The end." He started back toward his desk.

"Not so fast, Kreiser," the teacher said.

Henry stopped.

"Do you think you're smart?"

Henry shrugged.

"The assignment was two pages."

"I explained why I shortened it. I proved that science is not true."

"You proved nothing."

"I did so!" He shook his paper at the teacher. "Right here!"

"No. And you can't change the assignment. Is that fair to the others?"

Henry sat down at his desk.

"You'll complete the assignment by tomorrow," the teacher demanded.

Henry glanced at the teacher in the eyes then looked out the window, as if he didn't hear him.

"Oh, you won't do it? Well, you'll get an F if you don't."

"Stupid," Henry said, partially concealing the word with a cough.

The teacher got up quickly and walked to Henry's desk. "What's stupid?" he asked. He touched Henry's shoulder to get his attention.

Henry stood immediately, knocking the teacher's hand away. "This! This is all stupid!"

"Out! To the principal's office!"

"Tell me!" Henry yelled as he walked toward the door. "How did it begin? Lightning? Primordial soup? You believe that lightning zapped into a soup of chemicals and suddenly life started? You call yourself a scientist? Ask yourself these questions, because this all seems made up to me."

"Out!"

"Nobody understands. At least I understand *that*." Henry walked out and slammed the door.

All the students began to chatter about the drama. Sally stayed quiet.

By the time the teacher came out into the hallway Henry had burst into tears. The teacher shook his head and put his hand on Henry's shoulder. "Come on, buddy. Let's take a little walk."

At lunch the next day Henry found Sally was sitting alone. With his tray full of food he sat down across from her. She ate without looking at him.

"Sally?"

"What?"

"Will you go steady with me?"

She sighed and dropped her hands on the table— exasperated. "Henry. What's wrong with you?"

"What do you mean?"

"Can't you take a hint?"

His face flushed.

"Can't you tell I don't like you like that?"

"Like what?" Henry asked.

"Like somebody who wants to go steady. Anyway, I have a boyfriend."

"What?" Henry was astonished. "Who?"

"Tyrone."

"Tyrone!?" Henry looked around then leaned toward her. "He's black," he said in a hushed tone.

"Why does that surprise you?"

Henry became quiet. A silent fury built up inside of him. He got up and grabbed his tray to walk away, but then he stopped. He dropped the tray on the table, scattering his lunch, and pointed at her. "I did this all for you!"

She looked around. Some others were watching. "Shhh! Not so loud. What did you do?"

"Science class. Don't you remember? I wasn't very good in it. Now, I'm the smartest in the class."

"Oh really? You think you're the smartest in the class?" she asked, her voice growing louder. "Whoa! That's news to me. Well, congratulations! But I'm *still* not interested in you! And you're going to get an F anyway if your bad attitude continues!"

A black kid walked up and sat next to Sally. He looked at Henry, trying to understand the tension.

Henry ran out.

* * *

When the school year finished, Henry spent the summer wandering Hershey Park. He didn't go on rides, and he avoided the other packs of Milton Hershey kids.

In eighth grade, Henry, Donovan, and Sally were all in different sections. Henry kept to himself. His grades sank from A's and B's to B's and C's. He acted out in defiance often, as he believed he knew it all and wished to demonstrate that to the others. But most incidents were innocent, and just before his actions would get him in deep trouble, he would pull back, apologize half-heartedly and perform well.

One weekend in mid-winter some boys were running up and down the long hallway of Moldavia, hiding and seeking in the rooms. Two of the boys saw Henry enter the vestibule at the end of the hallway with a boom box and headphones in his hands. They approached the door to look in on him. When they peered in they saw Henry sit on the floor, plug in the boom box and take a brand new cassette out. It was Billy Idol's "Rebel Yell". There were floor to ceiling windows that looked out on a cornfield. Henry examined the cover of the cassette then took off the wrapping. But he stopped suddenly when he noticed the boys watching.

"Get out of here!" he yelled. He banged on the door scaring the boys away.

"He's mean," Henry heard one boy say to the other as they walked away. Henry put his headphones on and inserted the cassette. He tucked his hands under his legs to keep them warm. When the Billy Idol guitars and synthesizers started to soar, he sat back against the wall. He looked out as the brittle, broken cornstalks shook in the winter wind.

CHAPTER 5

Henry finished eighth grade in the spring of 1985. He packed his things in a few small boxes. When a van came, Mr. Kerning shook hands with the driver, a pudgy, red-faced man with a beard.

"Have you met Mr. McGlinchy, Henry? He's the dairy manager at your new student home."

Henry nodded. He loaded his boxes in the back.

As he drove away, Mr. McGlinchy looked in the rearview mirror. "Your brother is one of the best kids we have."

"Uh-huh." Henry stared off as they passed to the other side of town. They passed the chocolate factory and Hershey Park. Across from the golf course, they pulled down a long driveway, where a sign read "Union." Like Moldavia this student home was also ranch-style. But this one had a barn next to it and a pasture full of cows behind it.

In his new room Henry unfolded his clothes. He balled them into his new dresser.

"Life's different up here," Byron said.

"Yeah?"

"Got barn duty. Gotta wake up early for that."

"Yeah. I know." He put the boom box on his desk and pushed aside a cup with two pens in it.

"Well, what you don't know is, kids are tougher here. You were oldest down there but you're youngest now."

"I'm tough. I'm smart."

"Smart doesn't matter when you have skinny arms,

pimples, and glasses."

Henry slammed his drawer shut and left the room.

Late that night, Henry went to the bathroom. He looked in the mirror, took off his glasses, looked closely at his face and picked at a pimple. Then he put his glasses back on and flexed his skinny arm.

It was an early start in the morning. Bright lights were on inside, while morning dark was outside. In the barn, Byron gave Henry the master tour. Sixty cows stunk as they smacked their lips on steaming piles of silage. A dozen boys went through their routines mechanically. Some scrubbed udders with steamy, soapy water. Others piled hay on top of the silage.

Mr. McGlinchy walked in from another room. He looked down at a clipboard that rested on his belly. "Guys," he said, looking up. "Get those teats clean today! No shit in the milk, please!"

Henry laughed. McGlinchy shot him a nasty look.

"Come on outside," Byron said.

"Did he say tits?" Henry asked as they went out into the concrete lot.

"No. Teats... *teats*!"

Out on the concrete lot, a single bulb spread a thin light across piles of manure and illuminated a tall, white wooden fence lining the lot's edge. A truck's headlights moved in the dark along the road on the far side of the pasture. Henry and Byron stopped at a pit filled with liquid manure, from which a conveyor belt emerged.

"The conveyor scrapes all the shit from the barn out to here," Byron explained. "Then it gets dumped into that cart and spread on the fields. Any shit that falls off the conveyor will end up down there—in the pit. You *don't* want to get pit duty. It's the worst job in barn—for the bad kids. If you act up or don't work hard, that's where you'll end up." Byron looked Henry in the eye. "Whatever you do, you have to get Mr. McGlinchy's respect. He runs this place."

"Okay. I work hard," Henry asserted. He was sure of himself. "I clean good."

"But McGlinchy's tough."

"Okay. So am I. I'm smart."

"I know you are," replied Byron, "But I told you, smart doesn't matter. See how he looked at you in there?"

"How?"

"You laughed at the word teats. You need to grow up quick dude."

"Oh," Henry said. "Okay. So, I shouldn't laugh at tits."

"Teats! Now start scraping the lot. It's a first-day thing." Byron handed Henry a metal scraper.

"Wait ... I have to scrape that whole lot? Where does all the poop go?"

"Into the spreader with the rest of the shit from the barn... for the fields... get it done!" As Byron headed back into the barn, he turned to Henry. "And remember - it's shit, not poop!"

Henry started working. He was earnest and wanted perfection. The sun rose, but Henry's progress was slow. Scraping didn't come so easily, he found. He struggled, mishandling the scraper. He forced it and slammed it onto the concrete, until it finally broke in his hands. Mr. McGlinchy came out from inside the barn. "What have you done?!"

"Sorry ... it broke!" Henry held out the two parts of the scraper.

"I can see that. If the lot isn't cleared by the time we're done milking, we have a problem."

"I can't use this. Can I?"

"Over there is another," McGlinchy said.

Henry started to scrape again but moved slowly. His muscles quickly fatigued. Huge piles seemed unmovable. He stopped to take a break and leaned on the scraper handle.

McGlinchy poked his bearded face out the barn window. "You don't go down for breakfast until you're done!"

"But I'll never finish!"

"Don't 'but' me, boy. If I let the cows back out into a dirty lot, they sit down and get dirty teats. Then the other boys have to clean them. Do you want the other boys to be mad at you?"

Henry started scraping again. Twenty minutes later, the other boys left the barn. Some stopped to watch Henry struggle before going back to the house. A moment later, McGlinchy walked out with Byron.

"He's skinny," McGlinchy said to Byron, loud enough so Henry could hear. "Better thicken him up. Your brother needs to eat ... Oh, and, Kreiser, if he doesn't finish in time tomorrow, the lot is yours and he's going in the pit." McGlinchy looked over at Henry, who had stopped and was listening. "You're finished for today, Henry. Dirty teats it will be. Tomorrow, you *better* finish."

Byron shot Henry a threatening glance. "Yeah, I better not get the lot," he said.

Henry looked at the piles and clumps of manure that hadn't changed a bit since he started.

That evening, Henry organized his things as he settled in. He piled music cassettes next to his boom box. Byron came in with a basketball, in shorts and ready to hit the court.

"Put your play clothes on."

"Why?" Henry pulled open a cassette and straightened the paper sleeve inside.

"We're going to play ball."

"Nah," Henry said.

"Come on. You're on my team."

"My arms are sore. I'm just gonna listen to music."

"Come on! This is how you get to know the guys. You need to get on their good side from the beginning."

"No," Henry said, annoyed. "I don't want to."

Byron left the room, shaking his head in dismay.

When the morning light woke him, Henry moved his arms to pull the covers off and felt pain in his biceps and forearms. He felt them and they hurt to touch.

At the barn, the boys started the milkers on the inside as Henry took to the lot outside. Manure piles were now twice as high as they were the day before, and the cows had stamped them into hard, clotted piles. As he began, the scraper dominated his hands. It seemed heavier and was unmanageable. His sore arms were ineffective rubber bands. On first push, he felt blisters that had formed overnight. And within minutes, they burst painfully. When he saw a stripe of blood from a blister on the scraper handle his frustration grew. He looked through the barn windows and saw Byron, McGlinchy, and the others messing around and having fun as they performed their barn duties. He let out a frustrated sigh and slammed the scraper on the ground.

McGlinchy burst out of the barn. "What are you doing, Kreiser? You don't even want to try?!"

"My arms are sore! I have blisters!" Henry showed the palms of his hands to McGlinchy.

"Good. So you'll get stronger. Your hands will callous if you let them. Pick up the scraper."

"I'll never finish."

"You'll finish, or your brother has to help you!" McGlinchy started back toward the door.

Henry picked up the scraper and began to scrape again. "Ouch!" he yelled. He slammed the scraper down again.

McGlinchy turned. "Your choice!" He approached the barn door and called for Byron. "Kreiser, get your ass out here! You'll scrape the lot. Your brother's in the pit."

Byron came out. "Dumb-ass," he said to Henry. "I told you to stay on his good side."

McGlinchy came back with two buckets. "Over here," he told Henry. He took him over to the conveyor belt, which was dripping with manure. Under it was the pit—five feet deep and half full of liquid soup of manure from sixty cows.

"In *there?*" Henry asked.

McGlinchy handed him a bucket. Henry lowered himself into the muck, squeezing under the conveyor belt. Liquid manure came waist high, and the conveyor belt was so low that he had to stay hunched.

"I want it empty," McGlinchy said. "Clean. I should see the concrete bottom."

Henry started, but it was slow-going. His arms were so sore he could only lift half-full buckets.

Byron scraped the lot and finished in twenty minutes. Within another ten minutes, he had shoveled all the manure into the spreader. Putting down the shovel, he approached Henry and saw that little progress had been made. "You have to fill the buckets all the way because you lose some each time. I think you're working backwards."

"I can't pick them up. My arms are sore."

"Don't be a wuss." Byron went back into the barn.

Henry filled a bucket to the brim. He lifted it slowly and felt the pain. His arms shook. Then it slipped from his hands and plunged into the liquid manure. A splash reached his mouth and gave him a taste. It was on his glasses and speckled his cheek. Again, his frustration rose. He climbed out of the pit and found a hose nearby. Cool, clear water washed his mouth. It splashed his face and cleared his glasses.

McGlinchy rushed out. "What are you doing!? Back in the pit!"

"I got some on my face and my glasses. I can't see."

"Once in the pit, you stay in the pit until you're finished!"

Henry put his glasses back on. He lowered himself back in. Liquid manure was still waist-high.

McGlinchy now focused all of his attention on the impressionable, young Henry. He stood close by to watch. Henry started again, but McGlinchy's presence made him nervous. He banged his head on the conveyor and stopped again. He closed his eyes.

"What are you doing? Get to work!"

Henry breathed heavily, as if he was going to cry.

"You're not going to cry, are you?" McGlinchy asked.

"No." Henry wiped his eyes. "Just shit in my eye."

"Don't cuss."

"Oh my god," Henry said with a whiny tone in his voice. "Byron told me I should say 'shit' instead of poop now you're telling me the opposite?"

"Oh my god." McGlinchy mocked Henry's whiny tone.

"Well Byron has been working in the barn for two years. You just got here and have to earn the right to say 'shit'."

Henry started again as McGlinchy watched.

"Henry, have you ever heard of a black sheep."

"Yeah."

"Do you know what it is?"

"No."

"Well, I'm gonna tell you. Most sheep are white. The girls and boys in the flock have sex and make babies and sometimes a black baby is born. The flock unknowingly produces a black one to increase the likelihood that the whole flock will survive and pass on their genes. You see, the black one is bait. It's a weak one for the wolves. The wolves eat the weak one, so the rest of the flock goes on surviving."

"Yeah? I know about stuff like that. It's from evolution." Henry struggled with a full bucket.

Byron watched McGlinchy and Henry through the window.

"Yeah, smarty pants," McGlinchy said. "And you know what I think?"

"No. What?"

"I think you're the black sheep of your family. You have skinny arms. Your brother doesn't. You have bad eyesight. Your brother doesn't. You have crooked teeth. Your brother doesn't. You have pimples and he doesn't. You're bait for the flock. You are the weak, programmed to fail. That means others are going to single you out and pick on you. So it means you are going to have to work harder to show them that you're not the black sheep. You understand what that means?" McGlinchy reached out with his finger and flicked a wet piece of manure off a ledge.

The manure flew and stuck on Henry's glasses and in between his lips. Henry stared at McGlinchy and gritted his teeth. He spit the manure off his lips. He watched McGlinchy go in the barn and saw Byron watching from the window. *Piece of shit*, Henry thought. *Shit pile. Shit cow ass. McGlinchy. McFuckin Pinchy in the ass. Shit cow ass head*. Henry dipped the bucket down quickly. He yanked it back up. He dumped it. He dipped, yanked, and dumped fast now. He felt no pain. Twenty minutes later, the pit was empty.

The next day Henry woke up with aches and pains. And a fever soon arrived. He fell asleep and woke and fell asleep again. Byron came in and went out in the late afternoon. Henry's fever broke by evening.

Weeks later, on afternoon barn duty, Henry scraped the floor inside of the barn while other boys tended to the cows. Sucking air sounds and gurgles filled the air as the milkers sucked on the teats of a half dozen cows. The boys washed the udders of the other cows to prepare them for milking. "Watch out, Henry," one of the boys called. "Golden Arm is here!"

Henry looked around to see who he was talking about. At a stall near the end of the barn, McGlinchy was speaking to a man in a white coat. He held a long rubber glove out to the man and helped him pull it on his hand and then all the way up to his shoulder. After the man wiggled his fingers into the glove and pulled it tight, McGlinchy handed him a large syringe full of a white liquid. McGlinchy patted the man on the back with a smile and then held up a cow's tail. With his gloved fingers, the man searched the cow's backside. Through the hair and flesh, he found the spot. Then, he took the device in his gloved hand and shoved it and his arm deep inside of the cow's vagina, to his shoulder. Henry shuddered. He walked on to scrape the floor.

After the milking tubes quieted down and the cows had been chased out of the barn for the day, Henry hosed the floor, watching the water push the filth ahead and leave a trail of clean. McGlinchy watched him finish.

"Never see a cow get pregnant before?" McGlinchy asked. He leaned against the wall and threw his arm up on the window sill. He fiddled with the handle to the window.

"Uh ... no." Henry wrapped up the hose and unscrewed the nozzle.

"Do you know where to put that?"

"What?"

McGlinchy pointed to the nozzle in Henry's hand.

"The nozzle?"

"Yeah, your nozzle. Do you know where to put it?"

Henry looked at the nozzle, confused.

McGlinchy shook his head. "You don't get it do you?" He laughed and walked away. "We'll make a man out of you yet, boy," he called back.

Henry put the nozzle on the window sill and hung the hose on a nearby hook.

When they went back to the house, Mr. McGlinchy went to his apartment, a semi-detached structure at the back of the main house. As he went in, a teen girl with long brown hair, wearing a flannel shirt, came out. She nodded to Henry.

After showering, Henry went to his room and cracked the window. He sat by the window and smelled the sweet smell of July hay. He heard the wind blowing in the trees and began to make out the sounds of a heated conversation. He couldn't decipher any words, but he could tell a man, a woman, and a young girl were all involved. It sounded as if the man was angry and the young girl was pleading. The woman's voice seemed to be one of peacemaking. *McGlinchy*, Henry thought. *And the girl in the flannel. His daughter.* He lay down on his bed so his head was near the window. The conversation continued for nearly twenty minutes. It ended with a blurted statement by McGlinchy and a door slamming.

A faint sound of cowbells on the wind woke Henry before dawn. He looked up and saw his window was still cracked. Then he heard a man whooping and yelling. There was urgency and distress in the voice. Henry jumped out of bed and ran downstairs.

When he got out to the pasture in his barn clothes, Henry saw the glowing kernel of a cigarette moving back and forth. Then his eyes adjusted and he saw McGlinchy chasing the cows back up to the barn.

"Thank God you're here!" McGlinchy said when he saw

Henry. "Number forty-two slipped into the Swatara." He pointed down to a row of trees on the edge of a creek, barely visible in the morning dark. "Drive these cows into the barn then meet me down by the creek afterward! I'm going to get the tractor!"

"Yes sir!" Henry shouted like a good soldier. "I'll get them into the barn. I'll make sure every one of them gets in there. Then I'll meet you down there."

McGlinchy ran back toward the barn. Henry began whooping, yelling, and running back and forth as he drove the cows toward the barn. Minutes later McGlinchy zipped back down on the tractor. "Get the flashlight when you come down!" he yelled.

After he drove the cows inside to their stalls, Henry ran down to the creek with the flashlight. McGlinchy had backed the tractor down to the creek bank. Down below, the runaway cow stood with her hind legs stuck in mud and her front legs in the creek. McGlinchy was in the mud, trying to throw a strap around the cow's belly, when Henry slid down the muddy bank and splashed into the creek.

"Throw it over," Henry called.

"Hold on. We have to get it from around this side."

"Throw it over." Henry held his arms open wide. "I got it!"

McGlinchy threw the strap over the cow. Henry caught it in the air and yanked it. He pulled it down over the cow's back and threw it under to McGlinchy. After pulling the two straps together, McGlinchy hooked a chain up to the straps and ran up the bank. Henry followed.

As McGlinchy began to move the tractor forward, the cow mooed loudly in pain. Her feet came up out of the mud, and then the full weight of her body slammed into the muddy bank. Slowly, McGlinchy dragged her up to level ground. As he and Henry took the strap off, she flipped her body, threw her head, and popped up onto her feet.

"Get on," McGlinchy said, climbing back on the tractor and motioning to the frame behind the driver's seat.

Henry climbed up and stood behind McGlinchy. As the

tractor took off, Henry grabbed McGlinchy's shoulders.

By the time the cow, half-coated in mud, entered the lot, several boys were approaching from the house. Byron was there too. When McGlinchy drove the tractor into the lot, all saw Henry perched above him on the tractor, waving, with a big, proud smile on his face.

Later, while milking was in progress, Henry scraped the barn floors. He stopped often with the other boys to tell the tale of the cow in the creek.

"Good," Byron said, when Henry told him the story. "About time you earn your keep around here."

After hosing down the floor, Henry went into the milk house, a separate room with a big silver tank in it. McGlinchy was making notes on a clipboard. A loud motor was giving off a pulsing sound.

"You wanted to see me?" Henry yelled over the motor.

"I want to say thanks for this morning."

Henry smiled. He kicked at the stainless steel leg of the milk tank. "When I heard you out there yelling, I thought to myself, 'There is something wrong.' And, you know, I wasn't gonna just lie there in bed when you needed help."

McGlinchy turned a valve, and some milk passed through a clear tube into the big tank. Then he flipped a switch and the motor came to a stop. The room quieted. "Listen. Kids in ninth or tenth grade rarely get the opportunity to work the milkers. But I want you to get that rare chance. I have an offer for you."

"Okay."

"What do you think about getting up at 5 a.m. to drive the cows up from the pasture? You did such a good job down there this morning."

"Really?" Henry was excited. "Yeah. Yeah." He kicked the leg of the milk tank again. "Heck, yeah."

"Good. Then in a few months ... uh, maybe a year, you can start on the milkers."

* * *

AMERICAN SPAZ

From that day forward, Henry threw all his energy into barn duty and went far beyond what was expected of him. Each morning he woke up enthusiastically at five o'clock. He whooped and hollered to move the cows up into the barn. He even fed them their first meal of hay and silage before the other tired eyes arrived. And for every favor McGlinchy asked of Henry, he obliged. With a clipboard in hand, he took notes about the cows' udder sizes before and after milking. He swept the middle aisle between the two rows of cows. And going way beyond the call of duty, he bottle-fed newborn calves in the big open pen.

Byron, among others, became aware of Henry's new enthusiasm for barn duty. While Henry was in the calves' pen one day, Byron leaned on the railing and looked in. "What are you doing?"

"What do you think?" Henry held a full plastic milk bottle with a plastic teat. He darted after a calf, tackled it, and shoved the teat in its mouth. The calf screamed at first but then started sucking when it tasted the milk.

"I think you're being a brown-noser."

"Shut up. You're the one who told me to get his respect."

"You don't get somebody's respect by doing his job for him," Byron said.

"Well, you get respect by being helpful. Anyway, he told me that I could be on milker duty early if I help with this stuff."

"What? He said that?"

"Yeah. And he's gonna do it for me."

"No, he won't," Byron insisted. "He can't! He doesn't decide. Ninth and tenth graders don't do milkers."

"I don't care." Henry jabbed his index finger on the teat in the calf's mouth to get it to start nursing again.

"And now all the other guys think you're a brown-noser," Byron told him.

"I don't care what anybody thinks." Henry pulled the empty bottle from the calf's mouth and threw it aside. He grabbed another full one.

"Brown-noser!" Byron said as he turned away.

On Henry's first day at the high school, a grand old building with towers on a hill above town, he spent his time between classes wandering the halls. After exploring the academic halls in the front of the building, he went to the back of the building and watched boys going into carpentry, machine shop, and electrical shop.

In science class, the teacher, a red-haired, puffy-permed woman, paced around the room. She revealed the challenges for the coming year. She engaged each student with eye contact. Henry sat slumped in his chair. She stopped next to his desk.

"Kreiser, sit up in your chair."

Henry didn't.

Later that day, Henry went to the back of the school building to the machine shop, a big garage full of lathes, table saws, and wire wheels. The instructor, a man with a silver-haired flat-top, approached.

"I want to switch into this shop," Henry told him.

"What shop are you in now?"

"I'm not. I'm college prep."

"You sure you want to switch out of college prep?"

"I am."

The instructor stepped forward and grabbed Henry around the bicep. Henry's arm was so skinny that the instructor was able to wrap his hand all the way around it—until thumb touched index finger. "You should stay in college prep, young man."

Henry left the shop in a hurry and let the door slam behind him.

On Saturday, the changing room at Union was full of boys getting into play clothes. Most kids were putting on high-top sneakers and baggy T-shirts, but Henry slipped into a flannel shirt and dingy jeans.

"Why are you putting on barn clothes?" Byron asked.

Henry looked down at his shirt. "These aren't my barn clothes. They're my play clothes."

"Well, they look like barn clothes."

Henry shrugged. "Sorry. I don't dress like a black kid."

AMERICAN SPAZ

Byron looked around. A few other black kids nearby hadn't heard. "What did you say?"

"You heard me."

"Don't talk like that unless you want to get pummeled."

That afternoon, when the dozens of vans dropped off all the boys and girls at the main campus, most of them ran over to the baseball fields and basketball courts. The white-domed building presided over this part of campus. Henry walked across a wide-open, tall-grass field and down along a little creek. Frogs leaped into the water as he walked along the bank, kicking the grass. At the end of the creek, where it dumped into a manmade pond, he spotted a group of boys and girls under a patch of pine trees hanging around, and sitting on top of, two picnic tables. Most wore flannel shirts and worn-out jeans like Henry. As he approached, he saw one boy pass a cigarette to another.

One of the two nodded to Henry. "What's up, dude?"

"Hey, dude," Henry said.

Henry looked around at the dozen or so boys and girls. There were a couple of fat ones and a couple of skinny ones. Another had big ears. As two people moved away from the picnic table, Henry saw her sitting there. It was McGlinchy's daughter. He turned away from her.

"Henry?" she called.

He turned back to her. "Hey."

"I'm Patricia. Patricia McGlinchy." She got off the table and approached him.

"You're Mr. McGlinchy's daughter?"

"Yeah," she laughed. "Why are you acting like you've never seen me before?"

"You don't go here, do you? To Milton Hershey?" Henry asked.

"No. But I don't like the kids at the Hershey public high school, so I come here to hang out."

"She likes Milts," one of the other boys called, making kissing sounds.

"Shut up," Patricia said.

After some chatter, a burly kid with thin blonde hair and pale skin stood up to call attention to himself. "Listen in, everybody," he said, as if he had something important to say. "As you know, many people have started calling us 'pond people.' That's probably because we hang out here next to the pond, instead of over there, on the ball fields. They call us anti-social because we don't socialize with them. And they call us dummies because we're not in college prep."

"Tell it like it is Dearborn!" one boy yelled. "Who here wants Dearborn for class president?"

Others cheered in the affirmative.

"Ha ha. They'd never elect me and I wouldn't run anyway," Dearborn continued. "I don't care about them and you shouldn't either. We should all be proud to be pond people."

Some of the others laughed while some rolled their eyes to each other.

"If we went over to the ball fields then they would be calling us the ball field people. Right?"

Patricia stepped toward him. "Uh... no. They wouldn't, because the ball fields are all about sports, which is what they—"

"Patricia, my point is that we're different from them, and we shouldn't be concerned that they are calling us names. Like I said, we should be proud to be pond people. Be proud that we are different."

Patricia laughed. Henry saw Patricia laugh and then did so himself. He reached out to give her a light touch on the shoulder, but she looked at his outstretched hand, so he stopped. He touched his glasses on his face. He fiddled with the hair on the side of his head. Then he stepped forward to stand in front of the crowd. "I'm Henry Kreiser," he said. "I agree with Dearborn. We should be proud to be..." But Henry looked around and saw that the others had broken off into several unrelated conversations and weren't listening.

After Henry trailed off, Patricia pulled him aside. "Listen," she said.

"Yeah?" Henry blushed at the thought of her confiding in him.

"You can't tell my dad you saw me here."

"Of course not." Henry put his hand on his heart. "No. Okay. No. I won't say a word."

"Well, don't tell anybody else at Union either, okay?"

"I won't," Henry assured her.

"You promise?" She held out her pinky finger.

He grabbed her pinky with his. "Promise."

Dearborn pulled a boom box off the ground and put it on the table. When he pressed play on the cassette, a rock guitar screeched loudly. Henry watched in amusement as the other kids began playing air guitar and banging on the picnic table. Patricia, too, took part, stomping her foot to the beat and thrashing her hair.

At the barn that week, a black boy was hosing off the inside walkway while Henry used a broom to scrub the crud from the floor. Patricia walked in the door. Henry gave her a knowing look, made eye contact with her, but then pretended he didn't see her, relishing his secret pledge of silence.

"Where's my dad?" she asked the boy with the hose.

The boy stopped the water in the hose by making a kink. "In the office," he said.

She started to go in the direction of the barn office but then stopped. "Give me some," she said.

"What?"

"Give me some water." She leaned over toward the nozzle and parted her lips. She stuck out her tongue and opened wide.

"You ready?" the boy asked.

"Yeah! Give me some."

He released the kink in the hose and water shot out, hitting her in the eyes. She grabbed the nozzle and stuffed it in her mouth. He kinked the hose again.

Her mouth was full of water. It dribbled down her chin and wetted a clump of hair on her neck. She slowly pulled the hose from her mouth.

Henry dropped the broom.

"Sorry," the boy said. "I thought you were ready."

She swallowed the water in her mouth and then wiped off her lips with her fingertips. She smiled and walked on.

"Oh, my God," the boy said to Henry.

"What?" Henry watched her go into the office then picked up the broom.

"She is *nice*."

"Yeah. She is nice," Henry agreed.

"No. She's hot. You can't see it because she wears big flannel shirts, but her tits are huge."

"Really?"

"Yeah," the boy confirmed. "I mean, like, really big."

"She's my friend," Henry said suddenly.

"What?"

"I hang out with her. She's my friend. At the pond. We hang out. Smoke. You know? So—"

"She hangs out at the pond? McGlinchy's daughter?"

"Yeah. We hang out. I think she likes me, but I don't feel right about it."

The boy started hosing again. He laughed. "I can't believe she hangs out at the pond—with pond people. Wait 'til I tell the others."

"No. No. Don't. Don't say anything." Henry turned away from the boy for a second and let out a sigh of regret. He looked out the window. *Shit*, he thought. *My stupid big mouth.*

At school, during outdoor recreation, Henry was walking along with Dearborn and a couple other kids who were at the pond the past weekend. Henry tapped Dearborn on the arm and signaled for the attention of the other two. "Watch," he said. Henry ran forward toward a picnic table, yelling something incomprehensible, and leaped on top. His pond people friends watched and laughed as other students glanced over, not so impressed with Henry's antics. Henry jammed the air guitar then ran across the table, leaping through the air with the guitar. He landed on the ground in front of a black kid sitting on a bench with two twin white girls. It was Donovan.

"What's up, dude?" Henry said, surprised he landed

right in front of his old friend.

"*Dude?*" Donovan asked. "Since when do you use that word?"

The twins began talking among themselves, turning away from Henry.

"How are you?" Henry asked.

"Hanging out with the pond people now?"

"I asked: how are you?"

"You know, they're only trouble, those kids. You should stay away from them."

"I asked: how are you doing, Donovan?" Henry shook his head in frustration. "You know, there's a reason pond people are like they are."

"Oh, yeah? Why?"

"Because people like you make *us* that way."

"What does that mean?"

Henry shrugged. "Whatever." He walked away.

Donovan watched him walk back over to Dearborn.

The lunchroom in the high school was in the basement, lined with windows at the top of the walls. Feet passed by outside. Henry was sitting with two of his pond-people friends when Byron approached.

"We have to go to the principal's office."

"Why?" Henry asked.

"I don't know."

In the office Chuck, Kate, Teddy, and Liz were waiting.

"Hey," Henry said. "What are you—" He stopped short when he saw a sad look on their faces. For a second he felt off balance. Kate put her arm around his shoulder. Teddy put his hand on Henry's neck gently.

"What's going on?" Byron asked.

"Come with us," Kate said quietly. "Let's take a ride."

All were silent as Chuck drove down the hill from school. When they stopped at the traffic light, Kate turned in her seat to face them in the back. "Dad passed away this morning. At St. Mary's."

Byron gasped. Henry stared out the window at the parking lot, which was filled with antique cars.

Back at Union, Henry and Byron quietly packed their

bags. Byron held his tears back and kept an eye on Henry who, to Byron, seemed stuck in a blank stare.

At Kate's house in Levittown, they dressed themselves in their Sunday clothes.

In Langhorne Manor, a funeral home in a mansion on a corner across from a church, the six kids all lined up, from small to big, with the casket at the end.

Grandmom approached Henry first, while Mr. Cluskey stood back. She took Henry in her arms and burst into tears. "My dear, I'm so sorry. It must be so hard for you."

Henry nodded as he hugged her. He stared off at the flowers behind her.

Kate, who was standing behind Grandmom, looked at Henry's emotionless face and saw him staring off.

At Kate's house that night, the mood was somber. After eating and watching some TV, all went to bed. Henry woke in the middle of the night and went downstairs. He turned on the TV and flicked through the channels. He stopped on MTV and fell asleep to quiet music. He woke in the wee hours to a soft rock song. Billy Idol sang and danced. "Eyes Without a Face" was the song. Henry sat up. Billy Idol's face floated above a fire. Slow guitar reverberations sparked a pervasive feeling of sadness in Henry. He began to well up as if he would cry. Female vocals sang the chorus. Billy sang about no human grace; he sang with just his face. Henry went close to the TV and saw pain in Billy's eyes. But then the guitar changed and reverb went away. Billy fought back in the video, as if he no longer felt pain and found a new strength. Henry shook off the sadness he felt for a second. Guitar riffs soared high and hard and long. Henry got excited and jammed the volume high. He played the air guitar, and though he didn't know many of the lyrics, he pretended to sing along. When the chorus came, 'eyes without a face', he sang especially hard and loud. He jammed and sang with his eyes closed until the video's end, at which time he stumbled to catch his breath and opened his eyes. He was startled to see Kate there in her nightgown. He turned the volume down.

"Go to bed," she said. "It's late."

AMERICAN SPAZ

That Saturday at Hershey, after the other boys had gone out to play basketball, Henry slipped back into his room. He took a safety pin and some toilet paper from his pocket and set them on the dresser in front of the mirror. He quietly closed his door and took his glasses off. In the mirror he made tough-guy sneers and then looked closely at his left earlobe. He pinched it lightly then pinched it hard. Then he dug his nails in and ripped at it. He sneered again in the mirror and grabbed the safety pin, opening it. He pulled at his earlobe and plunged the pin through. "*Yeahhh!*" he screamed in pain.

Blood came quickly in little dribbles. He took the toilet paper and applied pressure.

Coming down from the barn on Saturday, Henry saw Patricia on her porch, playing with a puppy. He walked up to her, but she looked the other way.

"Hey," Henry said. She ignored him so he walked away.

Before he got far, he heard her call out, "Hey." She caught up to him and motioned to a spot between the carport and a bush. She pulled him over by his arm. "Did you tell somebody about seeing me at the pond?"

"No." He seemed earnest. "No, of course not."

She looked him the eyes. "Okay." She picked at the hedge. She looked at the ground.

"What's wrong?" he asked.

"Nothing. I just want to say ..."

"What?"

"I just want to say sorry about your dad." A tear came to her eye. She wiped it.

"Thanks." He touched her shoulder with his hand.

She grabbed his hand, squeezed it gently and looked closely at his ear, seeing the piercing hole. "Did you get your ear pierced?"

"Shh. Yeah."

"Cool. I bet you look cool with an earring."

"Yeah, I ... well, I guess I do."

When Henry got down to the changing room, he ripped his clothes off. *Patricia*, he thought to himself. *Pa-*

tri-cia. Patty. He laughed to himself as he ran into the shower. He soaped all his parts with vigor. *Delicious Patricious.* He laughed and threw the soap in the air.

* * *

In the following spring and summer, Henry saw Patricia often—always from afar, outside the barn window or on her porch. He listened from his window for her voice. Their little secret went unnoticed. Every time she ignored him, he knew it was her secret way of saying "I love you." It sent his heart aloft.

In Hershey Park, in August, Henry was with his pond-people friends. They met in the back of the arcade, where the ground sloped down to dumpsters and maintenance carts. Park staff in uniforms came and went. A couple of the boys were sneaking a smoke.

"Have you seen Patricia?" Dearborn asked Henry.

"Oh, yeah. See her all the time."

"At Union? Or at the pond?"

"Both. Sometimes we meet behind the carport," Henry said, proudly.

Everybody was suddenly focused on Henry.

"Really?" another boy asked.

"Yeah." Henry climbed up on a railing and looped his leg underneath.

"No. Really? You and Patricia McGlinchy?"

Henry nodded.

"I didn't think she was your type. I mean, I didn't think you were her type."

"What?" Henry asked, dismissively. "What is that supposed to mean?"

"Oh, nothing." Dearborn handed Henry a cigarette. "Did you touch her tits?"

"Yeah!" Henry declared.

"You're lying!"

"No I'm not. I swear."

"How big are they then?"

Henry put the cigarette in his mouth then indicated with his arms, like he was holding a bundle of logs. "So big. You would never know it because she wears those flannel shirts, but they're really big."

At that moment Byron walked by the front of the arcade with two other older kids. One of them stopped and pointed toward Henry. "Kreiser, is that your brother?"

Byron saw Henry up on the railing with the cigarette in his mouth.

When he saw Byron, Henry held the cigarette out in plain view, blew smoke, and then turned back to his friends. Byron shook his head in dismay and walked away.

In October, Henry and Byron were home in Levittown for the weekend. Kate and Jack were just a week out from their wedding and needed the boys home to get a final fitting for their usher tuxedos. It was also the night the bride and groom to-be were to go out for their bachelor and bachelorette parties.

"Come on," Henry begged Kate. "If Byron can go, why can't I? You're getting married."

"Even Byron is too young. But I can't tell an eighteen-year-old he can't do something. You're only fifteen though, Henry! No way!"

"It's just a bachelor party."

"In a strip club!" she exclaimed. "No!"

That evening Kate went to her own bachelorette own party before Jack left for his. When Byron got into the passenger side of the Jack's pickup truck, Henry ran outside and squeezed in.

"What are you doing here?" Jack asked.

"She said I could go," Henry said.

"No she didn't," Byron pushed Henry to get out of the car.

"Yes she did!" Henry grabbed onto the seat so he couldn't be pushed out. He closed the door. "I explained to her that I would stay out of the way and she was okay with it."

"You better not be lying to me." Jack searched Henry's

eyes for a lie.

They pulled the car into the parking lot of an old stone building. Flashing lights in red neon spelled out "Dancing Girls." As the three of them entered through a secret door on the side of the building, dozens of men – drinking beer in circles around the room – welcomed the groom-to-be with raucous cheers.

They grabbed Kate's fiancé and surrounded him with slaps on the back. "You've been a bad boy Jackie poo," one man whispered to Jack. "You're in for some punishment." Lights flashed to classic rock, casting shadows on the ankle-high stage. When the lights dimmed, a dark door opened in a corner.

A big guy in a flannel shirt handed Henry and Byron an orange-colored drink. "Vodka orange," he said. "Drink it. Your sister is marrying a great guy."

Henry took a sip, gave a gargoyle face, and gagged a bit. He sipped again. Two nuns stepped into the light on the stage—one had a dark complexion and black eyebrows while the other had lighter skin and red eyebrows. Henry was shocked and embarrassed when he saw them, sisters of the church, in that dimly lit den. He squinted his eyes to try to understand why they were there, and he looked to see the others, gathering around shushing each other. The nun with the dark complexion stepped forward smacking a ruler into the palm of her hand. "I'm Sister Hairy Mary, boys. And you have been very bad," she said, letting out a squeal of pleasure. She gave devilish grin and turned to the other nun. "We're going to have to punish you."

The light-skinned nun put her hands on her hips. "Do you know why they call me Nunalingus," she asked licking her lips, slowly. The men cheered and laughed. Henry laughed for a second then his face suddenly became contorted in disgust. His disgust, though, disappeared from his face immediately when the nuns turned to each other and embraced. As they began French-kissing and exploring each other with their hands—first over the habit and then up and under—Henry's eyes bulged. He froze and stared. Sister Hairy Mary's clothes fell quickly, revealing to

Henry's prying eyes curves and flesh he had only dreamed of before. She turned to Nunalingus, and fell to her knees.

The big guy patted Henry on the back. "Aha ha ha, good show!" he yelled over the music and cheering. "Finish your drink little man. Here's another."

Henry didn't take his eyes off the show. He downed one drink and dropped his plastic cup on the floor. What followed was the most inventive use of the mouth Henry had ever seen. Sister Hairy Mary used her lips and teeth to pull open the buttons on Nunalingus' habit as they both slowly and dramatically fell to the floor. By the time they lay on top of each other, both were completely naked. Men crowded closer and cheered. Excitement rose to the point that Henry's view was obstructed. He gulped the second cocktail and dropped his cup again. He squeezed up close to the stage and crouched down to get a better look. He kneeled right in front of the stage and watched from only inches away—his mouth gaping in disbelief. They had moved into the comfort of faked, mutual cunnilingus. He smelled perfume and other odors. Sweat stuck skin to skin as legs clamped on ears. Then, the theatric convulsions started.

A drunken man stumbled up and poked the top nun's butt.

"Stop!" Henry yelled, waving the man away.

The other men cheered Henry on. "The nerdy kid is drunk!" one yelled.

As the nuns continued, Henry's eyes bulged and then glazed in a disbelieving stare. He watched them climb up, kiss long again then help each other into their string panties. They started to dance together to rock and roll. They broke and turned to work the crowd. Dancing and grinding with the drunken men, the ladies received grabs and pinches. Men shoved their faces in bare breasts and stuffed crumbled dollars in the dancers' panties. Henry was a young man wild boy. He jumped from Sister to Sister, hoping for one or the other to fall in his arms. He danced with abandon—his eyes closed. Finally, when Sister Hairy Mary finished grinding with a man, Henry touched her shoulder.

"Nunalingus!" he yelled. "I love you!"

She turned to Henry. "I'm not Nunalingus honey. I'm Sister Hairy Mary." As she reached for Henry he stopped in his tracks as if he was suddenly afraid. But, out of nowhere, he felt a hand on his back—the big guy with the flannel shirt shoved Henry forward. And Henry pressed his young body against her womanly curves. As Henry breathed in her hair and reached his arms around her, the big guy turned to the others. "Future brother-in-law here!" he called out, causing them to erupt in laughter and crowd around Henry. She grabbed Henry around the shoulders and shook her hair to tease him. She danced around him. Henry grabbed her and pulled her close. He grabbed her legs and lifted her in the air onto his waist.

"Woooo! A wild one! Strong too." She blinked her eyes sweetly as she looked around at the others, putting on a show for them. She felt his little biceps. The men cheered wildly. Henry's hand roamed Sister Hairy Mary's backside and searched her upper thighs. He was drunk and dizzy in disbelief. He smushed his mouth on her cheek then lowered his face to search for soft flesh.

She stopped suddenly. "You're just a boy," she whispered in his ear. "It's just a show. I'm going to stop real slow. Just let me go."

"Okay. Sorry." He let her down slowly, not wanting to release her.

She stepped away. "That boy's a tiger," she said out loud. "Who's next?" Men gathered around. They pushed and shoved.

Byron slapped Henry on the back. "You done good!"

Henry looked at Sister Hairy Mary with a worried face.

"What's wrong," Byron asked.

"Tell her I'm sorry."

"Why?"

"I was rough. I tried to ... I tried to ... I touched her all over."

"Hey! Don't worry. That's what she gets paid to do. She's not really a nun. She liked it!"

Henry woke the next morning to screaming; it was Kate. He opened his eyes slowly and saw her feet. She was standing over him. He tasted carpet. He had slept with his mouth open, face down on the floor. He pushed himself up, cringing when his head spun and throbbed. On the floor in front of him was a partially dried pool of vomit.

"I can't believe you, Jack!" Kate yelled. "I told you very clearly that he wasn't supposed to go."

Jack's feet appeared in front of Henry. "But you weren't here," Jack defended himself. "And Henry told us you gave him permission to go!"

Henry saw Jack swaying but Jack wasn't swaying. "I'm sorry," he said, then gagged and threw up on top of his throw-up.

Despite the bachelor party debacle, Jack and Kate's wedding the following week was a momentous celebration. The ceremony took place in a catering hall in northeast Philadelphia. Families from both sides of the aisle—mainly of Irish and German descent—celebrated into the wee hours in joyous revelry. They danced, sang and toasted to good health. Henry didn't touch the alcohol, but he did do the Hokey Pokey with grandmothers and young kids. At one point, the big guy who had given Henry the drinks at the bachelor party gave him a wink.

Back at Hershey, Henry walked into the barn and picked up a clipboard from a window sill. "Assignments" was written at the top. He found his name and slammed the clipboard back on the desk. He found Byron sitting on a railing on the other side of the barn.

"McGlinchy still hasn't put me on milkers!"

"I told you, he can't. It's not his choice. He's manipulating you, Henry."

As Henry grabbed the scraper, he stared through the office window at McGlinchy, who was seated at his desk. McGlinchy caught Henry's stare in his peripheral vision, and then stared back at him. He waved and smiled to Henry.

Shortly after Henry left the barn that afternoon he saw

Patricia in the space between the carport and the bush. Her face was in her hands. He ran to her.

Her eyes were red and swollen. "He hit me." She grabbed Henry's hand.

"What? Who?" Henry puffed up with a sense of gallantry and looked around.

"My dad. He smacked me in the face." She pulled him close to her.

"Why'd he do that?" Henry embraced her.

"I don't know. I went to the milk house just now, and he told me to never come to the barn again. Then he hit me."

"Oh my fuckin' God" Henry glanced up toward the barn. "That's it! I'm done with him!" He ran back up toward the barn.

"No!" she called. "Stay here with me!"

Henry stormed into the milk house. McGlinchy was taking notes on a clipboard.

"I'm done!" Henry yelled.

McGlinchy put the clipboard down on a shelf. "Done with what?"

"With doing all this extra stuff. I'm still not working the milkers like you promised."

"You will soon. Next year."

"Yeah. Well, everybody else in my grade will too. So why did I do all this extra work?"

"Henry, I told you. You're gonna have to work a little bit harder than the rest of the kids."

Henry kicked the milk tank. He pointed at McGlinchy. "No. That's a lie. You're a bad person, Mr. McGlinchy."

"What did you say boy!?"

"No. I'm not gonna wake the cows. I'm not gonna feed the calves. I'm not gonna be your slave anymore! And you shouldn't hit Patricia." Henry left and slammed the door.

On the following day when Henry arrived in the barn, McGlinchy asked Henry to follow him. They went up to the dark, dusty, cavernous area of the barn, where the hay, straw, and grain was stored.

"I want you to move all that hay over here. We need to

make room for the coming harvest."

There were thousands of bales of hay, stacked nearly fifty feet high.

Henry accepted his task but was quietly livid. He climbed to the very top and began working furiously, throwing bales thirty feet down to the floor where they broke open. He worked like this for the first couple of days.

On the morning following the third day, he lay in bed before the light went on. He touched his arms. They were sore to the touch. But then he really felt them. He wrapped his hand around one. He got out of bed and turned on his light. In the mirror, he flexed his arms like a bodybuilder.

Byron rolled over in bed and put his face under his pillow. "What are you doing?"

"My biceps are pumped the freak up!"

When he started moving the hay that day, he lifted slowly and felt his arms work. He curled each bale like a barbell. He lifted them onto his chest, pressed them up above his head, and carried them to their new spot. At one moment, when he was on top of a stack near the ceiling, he heard somebody enter. He dropped the bale of hay. "Who's there?"

Patricia stepped into the dusty light. Henry sat down and rolled his sleeves up onto his shoulders, revealing his hard little biceps. She climbed up and sat down on the hay next to him. "What did you say to him?" she asked.

"Just told him I'm not gonna do him any more favors."

She took off her flannel shirt, lay back, and looked at the ceiling. Henry took the opportunity to examine her from head to toe. He saw the breasts, locked his gaze on them for a second, and then looked away.

"Thanks," she said. She sat back up and pulled his ear to turn his face. They stared at each other for a very long moment. Henry began to breathe heavily.

"What's wrong?" Patricia asked.

"Noth ... noth ..." He leaned forward with his face toward hers. And she was ready to receive his lips. But then his hand shot out at the same moment. He grabbed her left breast and squeezed it.

She screamed and slapped his face. "What are you doing?" She got up and grabbed her flannel.

Henry's face turned to stone. "I ... I ... I don't know. I thought ..."

"You thought you could touch my tit? You think I'm a cow?"

"Yes! I mean no! Of course I don't. I thought you liked... I thought you wanted to kiss."

"No, Henry. I didn't. I just came to tell you thanks for telling my dad off. That's all. But forget it now." She climbed down and walked out.

Henry sat still for nearly twenty minutes, uttering a single word over and over in his mind. *Fuck*, he thought. *Fuck. Fuck. Fuck.*

When he finally got up, he ripped down hundreds of bales of hay in a short amount of time, leaving a huge pile of broken hay bales in the middle of the floor. Then he walked out.

In the wee hours of the morning, Henry tossed and turned endlessly in bed. Eventually, he got up, got dressed, climbed out his window, and snuck past the carport. As soon as he reached the driveway near the barn, he started to run. A truck passed on the road across the way. He ran across a steep gully and climbed up onto the road. *I can't believe I fucked it up*, he thought as he started running on the shoulder.

He sprinted with all his strength. He passed darkened orchards and cornfields, and then, when he saw the lights of a shopping center up ahead, he stopped. He could barely breathe. He saw a K-Mart and some other stores. It appeared from a distance that a 7-Eleven was still open, so he continued walking to the shopping center, as he caught his breath. He went into the store.

"Camels," he said to the cashier.

The cashier, an old man, took a hard look at him. "How old are you, young man?"

"Eighteen."

"No, you're not."

"Yes, I am," Henry leaned forward and put a serious face expression on his face. "I'm getting them for my mom anyway."

"Do you have a note?"

Henry shook his head.

The phone rang, so the cashier turned and walked to the back counter to answer it.

Henry reached up behind the counter and grabbed a random pack of cigarettes. He then grabbed a pack of matches from a nearby box and ran out.

"*Hey!*" the cashier yelled, as he ran around the counter and out the door.

Henry sprinted across the street and jumped behind a bush. He opened the cigarettes and watched the cashier.

"Hey! I see you behind the bush! You Milton Hershey kids are nothing but trouble!" The cashier went back in the store.

Henry walked off the road and into the shadows of an orchard. He began to think about Patricia—her hair and her curves. He thought about lying in the grass with her and holding her close. He lit a cigarette and sucked it down quickly. Then he lit another. He lit and smoked one after another as he wandered in the general direction of student home Union. Some of the cigarettes he finished, while others he just smoked a couple puffs of before casting aside. But the farther he got into the pack, the less he thought about Patricia, and the more he was distracted by a deep hurting inside his belly. It started as a warm uneasiness but quickly turned into a raging fire. Henry stopped and grew dizzy. He was near an apple tree and was suddenly not sure which way was home. Then the fire in his stomach exploded, and vomit shot out of his mouth. He had no choice but to drop to his knees and let it fly. After a few minutes, his stomach had expelled all the liquid and the convulsions slowed. Then there were a few dry heaves. Only a dribble was left on his chin. He wiped it. After he gathered himself, he pulled the pack of cigarettes out and threw it to the ground. He stamped on it angrily and walked away.

He spotted the road in the distance so continued walking. When he got back near Union, there was a dim blue light on the horizon. He heard the cowbells and McGlinchy's tired whoop and holler. He snuck back in the shadows through the carport to his window. Before he climbed back into his bedroom, he looked at his sleeve in the dawn light. He gasped at the sight of blood on it. He panicked, scrambled back in the window and woke up Byron immediately.

Byron looked at his clock. "Oh, don't wake me up at this hour. I have twenty more minutes."

"Wake up. I think I'm ... I'm bleeding. Oh my god!"

"What!?" Byron sat up and turned on his desk light. "What are you talking about? What's that smell?"

"Smoke. I was smoking."

"You were not."

"I was... I went out. I ran out, and I went to 7-Eleven. I stole cigarettes and smoked most of the pack. But now, I'm paying for it. I threw up blood Byron. I'm bleeding on the inside."

"Oh my God! Sit down. When did this happen?"

"Just now." Henry sat down on his own bed. "Twenty minutes ago, as I was walking back... I'm dying!"

"You're not dying. But we should think about waking somebody up."

"Wake them up!"

"How do you feel now? Beat on your chest. How do you feel?"

"I feel ... I feel like I'm going to ... I feel fine, actually."

"Okay. Just sit there. Don't move."

Byron turned off his desk light, lay his head back down, and fell asleep instantly. When the lights came on, Henry was still awake. He was lying back on his bed, looking at the ceiling.

"You're fine," Byron said.

Henry got up and looked at the blood on the sleeve of his flannel. He ripped the shirt from his body, popping all the buttons. He balled it up and stuffed it under his mattress.

"You're an idiot, Henry."

"I know."

"Don't 'I know' me. You're stupid. What's wrong with you?"

"I learned my lesson," Henry said. "I'll never smoke again."

"What about stealing? You want to go to jail?"

Henry shrugged.

"You do?"

"No! Of course not. I regret it."

"Well, it's not just this. You've been acting stupid for a long time; hanging with pond people, telling people you are going out with Patricia. You gotta stop this shit, or they're gonna kick you out of the school."

"Well, I *want* to leave school! That's what I'm gonna do. When you graduate, I'm done. So they can't kick me out. So I don't care."

"You're not getting out. You're gonna graduate from Milton Hershey."

"No. I tell you, I'm leaving."

Byron shook his head. "Why can't you just be normal? Play sports with guys. You know, participate."

Henry got up, quickly opened his closet door, and then slammed it. "Because I'm *not* normal! People treat me differently from you. Haven't you noticed?"

"Don't yell...calm down!" Byron stayed quiet as he finished getting dressed. "I'm sorry," he said finally. "But I told you when you came here that you needed to get rid of the glasses. They make you look geeky, but you really aren't. And you need to put on some weight. If you do those two things, people will treat you differently. You'll even get chicks."

Henry continued moving the hay in the barn each day. He was sluggish at the beginning of the first day. Then, toward the end that day, as his muscles fatigued, he began to think about the physical aspect of his work.

While in the shower that evening he slicked up his skin with soap and examined his arms and chest with his hands. He was able to differentiate his biceps from the tendons that connected his biceps to his forearm. His muscles were sore but the tendons were not.

When he went out the second day he took a new approach to moving the hay, lifting and placing the bales in a deliberate and controlled manner – in a way that would make his muscles flex and burn. And over the course of that week, by focusing his attention on his muscles, he cleared his mind of any lingering concerns he had about Mr. McGlinchy or Patricia. In fact, they never even entered into his thoughts. By the time he was finished moving all the hay a month later, Henry had achieved a sort of nirvana—a physical euphoria that dispelled his emotional hang-ups. And though he was in reality still a skinny young man, he believed his biceps and shoulders were Herculean. For Henry, in those moments, nothing else mattered.

CHAPTER 6

Henry was doing push-ups on the floor of the bedroom when Byron walked in.

"Straighten your back," Byron said.

"I like it like this," Henry said as he pushed up and down fast with his mid-body hanging close to the floor.

"Slower," Byron said.

"I like to do it fast." Henry was running out of breath.

When he was done he got up. "Dinner!" he exclaimed, as he ran out.

At dinner Henry scooped himself extraordinarily big piles of meat and potatoes. The other boys all looked at his plate.

"You have a tapeworm, Kreiser?" one asked. "Where's all your food going?"

Henry shot the boy a look and flex his bicep for him.

Kate came to Hershey on a Saturday and took Henry and Byron to the shopping mall in Harrisburg.

"You each get one thing," she said.

Henry chose a pair of mirrored aviator sunglasses. Byron chose a new pair of basketball shorts. Henry put on his sunglasses over his eyeglasses as they walked through the mall. At one point, while Byron was inside a store, Henry and Kate stood near the fountain, throwing pennies in the water.

"I'm done with Milton Hershey," Henry said.

"Huh?"

"Can you take me out and let me go back to public

school?" he asked.

"What? Why?"

"I don't fit in. I need more freedom."

"Milton Hershey is good for you," she argued, gently.

Henry sniffled and rubbed his eyes behind his two pairs of glasses.

Kate looked at him. "What's wrong."

"I just want to be back ... I want the family ... I don't want to be here all by myself after Byron leaves."

"But it's best if you stay here—for you."

"If you take me out, I promise I'll be good. I'll do so good at school in Levittown. Please. Please take me out of this stupid school."

Kate put her arm around Henry's shoulder as he threw the whole handful of pennies into the fountain.

At recreation, Henry avoided the pond people altogether. He dressed in the more nondescript school-issued clothes and blended in willingly with all the other kids. One day he ran into Donovan in the school hall.

"Been lifting?" Donovan asked.

Henry shook his head. "No, why?"

"You're looking a little thicker."

Henry looked down at his arms. "Really?"

Byron arrived and smacked Donovan on the back. "We're gonna squash you guys, Donovan," Byron said.

Donovan reached to smack Byron in jest causing Byron to flinch. Henry laughed.

"You playing?" Donovan asked Henry. "Want to get beat?"

"Nah," Byron said. "Henry's too cool for basketball,"

"I'll play," Henry said.

"No, you won't," Byron said. "Your pond-people friends will make fun of you."

"I don't hang with them anymore. I swear. I'll play."

Henry played basketball from that day forward. When the other kids at Union met on the outdoor courts to practice for intramural basketball, he was there. And even though he was chosen as a second- or third-string player, he provided support from the sidelines. Being interested in basketball allowed Henry to see how good of a player Byron was, and more importantly, how much respect he got from his peers as a result. Byron's moves were not only effective for winning games, but they were also fancy – he would pass the ball behind his back, bounce it between his legs before making a shot, and, most astonishingly, he would take hook shots from way outside. Henry was inspired.

When he finally got asked onto the court one Sunday, he stayed out of the middle and avoided contact with the ball. But then suddenly, at about mid-game, an opposing player threw a bad pass, and the ball landed on Henry's chest. He paused. There was nobody in between him and the net.

"Take it up," one of his teammates called.

"Kreiser Junior has the whole net to himself," somebody called from the sidelines.

"Go," Byron yelled.

Henry shot forward, dribbling the ball. As he approached the net, he threw his leg forward to bounce the ball between his legs before shooting. It was a fancy move he saw Byron make before. But the ball hit his foot, and he fell forward onto his face. As he slammed and rolled onto the ground, his glasses flew off. Everybody laughed, and there was an especially loud grown-man's laugh. He popped up, put on his glasses, and saw Mr. McGlinchy and Patricia laughing at him.

"Game over!" A tall black boy who was on the first string lineup grabbed the ball and moved to the middle of court. "All right, guys. We got a good team now. First string and second string. So now we need a theme song to play before each game. I have an idea." He motioned to another boy behind the net. The boy pressed play on a boom box. A song started, with piano notes slow and spaced. After a few measures, an earnest, passionate voice began to sing. Bill Withers sang "Lean on Me." It was first a song about pain and sorrow but then turned optimistic, about moving on and tomorrow.

Henry, still angry that McGlinchy and Patricia were laughing at him, jumped in the middle with the tall kid and started dancing to the music—twirling his hands in the middle, and then throwing one arm in the air. He repeated the twirl and then threw the other arm up in the air. The others laughed at Henry and came into the middle to mimic his moves. "Lean on Me" continued—the chorus brought an offer to help a person carry on—and a friendship for all time.

* * *

In the coming weeks the Union crew took on other student homes. Henry didn't play at all but was fully engaged and became especially excited when Byron scored. Game by game, Union won and won again. Each game was started with and followed by the Union crew's playing of "Lean on Me." And the dance Henry had invented became a ritual that all team members participated in.

Henry was scraping the walkway during afternoon barn duty when he saw McGlinchy struggling with a bale of hay. He watched McGlinchy pull the hay bale up onto his stomach and drop it back to the ground before kicking it in frustration. Henry laughed to himself and looked around at the others. "McGliiiiinchy!" he said loudly, so others could hear. "Why don't you come out onto the court one day? Me and Byron pick a team, and you pick your team."

McGlinchy stood. He kicked the hay bale again. He straightened his shirt over his belly as the other boys stopped to watch.

Henry stepped into the aisle. He grabbed an imaginary basketball, took a shot in McGlinchy's direction and paused to watch it go in the basket. "Yeah. Me, my brother, and three others. You pick your team. I bet we take you down!"

"Ha! You got it punk," McGlinchy said. "How about

tonight?"

Henry nodded. "Game on" He squeezed his genitals and, with an exaggerated strut, walked over to grab the scraper. The other kids laughed.

"Henry Kreiser called you out, McGlinchy!" someone shouted.

McGlinchy shot Henry a nasty look. "You black now?"

The other boys stopped laughing.

"I dare you to take it to the net, McGlinchy. I smack you down," Henry said, causing the others to erupt in laughter again.

That evening, the five on five game was on under carport lights. It was Henry, Byron, another white kid, and two black kids. On the other side was McGlinchy, two white kids, a wide-shouldered Latin kid, and the tall black kid. Byron played the court and took on McGlinchy with some fancy moves. He scored again and again. When the black kid switched with McGlinchy, he slowed down Byron's scoring spree. At one point, Byron passed the ball to Henry on the open court. Henry shot, but it missed the backboard and fell into the bushes. McGlinchy laughed loudly, with aggression, and slapped his knee.

Then, McGlinchy brought the ball down court directly at Henry and moved inside. Henry moved to block him but tripped allowing McGlinchy to lay it up and miss. Byron grabbed the ball and played it back down the court. McGlinchy caught up and stepped up to defend his net. But a head fake by Byron sent McGlinchy flying off in the wrong direction. Byron scored. McGlinchy gathered himself, ran back, and punched the metal backboard pole. "Fuck!" he struggled to catch his breath. "Somebody block Kreiser!"

McGlinchy took the ball down the court, and Byron stole it. He passed it to a teammate, who passed it to Henry.

"Lay up!" Byron yelled.

Henry had the net to himself so put the ball up gently. It slid off the backboard and into the net. His team went wild and congratulated him with back slaps. Henry stood tall, picked up the ball from the ground and held it out as if he was going to hand it to McGlinchy. But instead he dropped it at McGlinchy's feet. McGlinchy saw red. He kicked the ball hard and grabbed Henry by the shirt—shoving him and yanking him until Henry flew backward onto his butt and slammed the back of his head on the asphalt. Henry's eyeglasses flew off and skipped across the court.

Stunned, everybody stopped and looked at Henry then at Byron, waiting for a reaction. "What the fuck did he do that for?" the black kid asked Byron.

Byron, red-faced in anger, ran up to McGlinchy. "Why'd you do that?!"

The door opened on the McGlinchy's porch, and Patricia came running out toward the court. As she approached, McGlinchy pointed at her. He motioned for her to go back in the house. She ignored him and helped Henry up.

"Why'd you do that?" Byron asked again.

"He dropped the ball at my—"

Byron threw his fists together into one and shoved against McGlinchy's chest. McGlinchy teetered for a second then slammed back on his butt. McGlinchy rolled over onto his belly, but then pushed himself up quickly and began pacing back and forth.

Patricia handed Henry his glasses as McGlinchy glared at her and she back at him.

In the end, Henry escaped punishment, but Byron was put on 5 a.m. duty for a week. Down at the pasture each morning, he whooped and hollered to bring the cows up.

Student home Union easily dominated the first half of the championship game. At the start of the fourth quarter, with a fifty-point lead on the boards, the Union starters stepped aside and let the others play. Henry was on the court. He and the other younger kids were much less skilled and missed almost every shot. The opposing student home scored at will, but the lead was too wide to make a difference. In the final seconds of the game, Henry dribbled the ball outside the arc into three-point range. With three seconds left, barely looking at the net, he hooked the ball high into the air. The ball hung in the air for a moment, eliciting cheers from the spectators, before it nipped a rafter and then slammed down into the bars behind the backboard.

To celebrate their win the Union boys put on their final show. With "Lean on Me" on the boom box, they did their signature synchronized dance: right hand up to the sky, twirled their hands in the middle, then left hand up to the sky. At one point Henry took it all in—black boys, white boys, Latin boys. He closed his eyes and sang along.

One evening Henry was preparing for bed as Byron made karate moves in the mirror with his shirt off. With each punch, kick, and chop he uttered a loud "Eeeyah!" Henry laughed as he got in bed. But then Byron went on the attack so Henry threw his arms up in defense.

"Take your shirt off," Byron said.

"Why?"

"I wanna show you something."

"What?" Henry asked.

"Just take your shirt off."

Henry took it off.

"Any time you get in a fight, take your shirt off," Byron said. "Otherwise, somebody will pull it over your head and pummel you. Now grab my wrist." He held his hand out.

"Why?"

"Just grab my wrist!"

Henry grabbed it loosely.

Byron flipped Henry's hand and yanked it in. Henry stumbled forward and tried to pull away. But Byron continued his attack, chopping Henry's arm and knocking him further off balance. Before Henry could make any sense of the situation Byron's forearm slammed across his head. Henry nearly fell, and his glasses were knocked cockeyed on his face.

"Why did you do that, butthole!?" Henry caught his balance and fixed his glasses.

"I'm learning karate, so I'm gonna teach you."

"I don't want to learn."

"Then why were you doing push-ups the other day?"

Henry shrugged.

"Well? Why?" Byron asked.

"I just want to not be so skinny," Henry said. "That's all."

"But *why*?" Byron persisted.

"Just because."

"You were doing push-ups because you want to get stronger so you can defend yourself."

"No!" Henry said.

"You want McGlinchy to continue picking on you? Or do you want to put a line in the sand and show him that you won't take it anymore?"

"Neither. I don't care."

"Well, I'm not gonna be around to defend you for the rest of your life, Henry."

"Shut up. I don't need you to defend me."

"You do if you don't learn to defend yourself."

Henry shook his head. "I don't like to hit people."

"Neither do I. But sometimes people need to be hit. Like McGlinchy."

Three kids in pajamas stopped in the Kreisers' doorway to watch. Henry looked at them. Then he took off his glasses and set them down. He pointed at the ceiling. When Byron looked up, Henry snatched his wrist. But once again, Byron flipped his hand over, grabbed Henry's hand, yanked him in, and smacked his forearm against Henry's head. He threw Henry to the floor with ease.

"Asshole!" Henry shouted.

"Hit me!"

"No, Byron. Leave me alone!"

"But you have to learn to defend yourself!"

"No, I don't!" Henry got up, opened a drawer and slammed it shut. He opened it again and slammed it again. "Mom taught me to never hit anybody!" he yelled. "She taught me to turn the other cheek."

Henry slammed the door on the kids who were watching. He jumped in bed.

That week McGlinchy approached Henry in the barn. "Your time has finally come," McGlinchy told Henry. "I want you on milker. Go grab a bucket of soap and water."

"Really?" Henry put down the scraper and grabbed a bucket of soapy water.

As McGlinchy watched, Henry stood behind the cow, an especially dirty one, and sopped the filthy, pink flesh of the udder with the rag. He gently wiped each teat, rolling them around to get them clean. In doing so he only made it dirtier, smearing the caked manure into mud that now coated the udder and teats.

"You have to scrub," McGlinchy pointed at the udder. "Get in there. You ever hear of a little elbow grease Kreiser!?"

Henry bent down closer and scrubbed harder.

McGlinchy pushed Henry's arm. "Scrub! Harder! You'll never get that dirt off."

Henry tried to follow the instructions, but McGlinchy had forced him into an angle from which he had no leverage. Then McGlinchy nudged him in even closer to the cow. Henry almost fell so he stood for balance, and McGlinchy shoved him harder still. Henry tipped forward as he tried to stand up, and his nose and cheek smeared against the dirty, manure-sopped hair on the cow's butt.

Henry snapped. He turned suddenly and knocked McGlinchy's arm away. He followed that with a push to the chest that knocked McGlinchy off balance. As McGlinchy struggled to get back on two feet, Henry slammed a fist into his chest. McGlinchy fell hard, banging his head on the wall and slamming his butt onto the ground. Henry leaped forward and stood over him. He looked directly into McGlinchy's eyes and grabbed him by the neck. He cocked his fist back.

"Yo, yo, yo, yo!" somebody yelled. A milker hit the floor and sucked loud in pulses. "Kreiser, your brother!"

Byron and two other kids ran to the end of the aisle, where they could see Henry standing with his fist clenched above McGlinchy. Henry backed off.

McGlinchy rolled over and pushed himself up. He

touched the back of his head and looked at a spot of blood on his hand. "In the milk house," he told Henry as he walked away. "Back to work!" he yelled at the others.

When Henry entered the milk house McGlinchy was looking at a meter on a clear tube through which milk flowed. Henry walked up next to him. "I'm sorry."

"Don't be sorry. You are who you are."

"What do you mean?"

"I mean you're the black sheep. You've just proven that to me and everybody else."

Henry watched the milk flow.

"Your brother graduates in a month. Maybe you should leave too."

"I was planning on leaving anyway." Henry turned to walk away, but McGlinchy grabbed his shoulder with a threatening grip.

"And don't you *ever* go near my daughter again."

Henry shook McGlinchy's arm off and ran out.

By the end of the following week Henry was sitting in the dean's office in the administrative building next to the domed building.

"You know your barn officer is being fired," the dean said. "You're not the first kid he's picked on. And he had no right suggesting you leave the school."

"He didn't pick on me."

"Well, I'm officially asking that you stay with us, Henry. You've been an exceptionally good student. Grades and attitude dipped a little over the past two years, but we understand ... with your dad's passing. We want you to have the best possible chance when you go out into the world."

"I'm ready to go out in the world now."

At lunch that day Donovan found Henry by himself at an empty table toward the back of the room. He sat down in front of him.

"Don't even think about leaving the Milt," Donovan said.

"What ... who told you?"

"I can just tell."

"Byron told you?"

"Yeah. And I understand why you want to leave." Donovan started eating his tuna casserole.

Henry finished eating. He put his fork and knife across his plate. "Why do you think I want to leave?"

"I think you got used to having your brother around and feel strange being here without him."

Henry nodded. "Yeah. I guess."

"But you should know I feel like your brother too, man. And you can rely on me like I am."

"Thanks man. But I gotta move on. I'll keep in touch."

After the seniors at Milton Hershey graduated, and threw their hats in the air, the celebrations began. While most undergraduates anxiously waited for exams to finish and for summer to start, Henry was already feeling the same freedom as Byron and the other seniors. He barely thought about exam questions and scratched in answers randomly.

He was walking through the hall on the final day of exams when Dearborn approached him.

"Congratulations, Dearborn," Henry said.

"Thanks, dude. I hear you're getting out."

"Yeah. You know... moving on."

"You're fucking lucky man—the real world with the rest of us! Listen, a bunch of us are having a party at the Chocolate Motel tonight. Someone wants you to be there." Dearborn winked. "If you know what I mean..."

"I don't know. You know... I have nothing against you guys, but I'm just onto different things."

"It's Patricia."

"Patricia? She wants me there?!"

Henry walked out through carport in his play clothes that night. He crossed the gully and went up the road, where Dearborn was waiting in a car for him.

When they arrived at the motel, music pounded from one of the rooms. Henry looked in with Dearborn and saw graduates dancing around a keg of beer. Somebody was flashing the light off and on to create a strobe effect. Henry started to walk into the party but Dearborn grabbed his arm.

"She's waiting in my room," Dearborn said. "That one."

Henry knocked and walked in. Patricia was there on the bed, propped up on the pillows. "Want a piece of gum?" she asked. "Give you fresh breath."

Henry sat down on the bed with her. Then he lay back on the pillows. They chewed gum as they looked into each other's eyes. After ten minutes, she took a deep breath. "Are you gonna kiss me?"

Henry moved in immediately. They kissed with wide open mouths—tongue swam with tongue. They traded gum. Then she reached for his hand and put it up under her shirt. He felt no bra. He spun in excitement. He stopped kissing and moved to explore her body with hands and face—marveling at the size and shape of the flesh he found. But a knock on the door stopped him. She pulled her shirt down. "Come in!"

Dearborn looked in. "You done?" he asked.

"No," Henry said.

"Yes," she said.

"Let's go, Kreiser. I need to take you back before I get drunk."

Henry lay there next to Patricia. He shot Dearborn a dirty look.

"Come on, man," Dearborn said.

"You don't want me to go," Henry asked Patricia. "do you?"

She patted him on the head. "Go now. Have a nice life."

"But I thought this was it. Like when we..."

"When we what Henry? I hope you didn't think we were going to..."

"No. No, of course not."

Henry slid off the bed and stood in the doorway with Dearborn. "I'll probably have my own car and stuff," Henry said to Patricia. "So, you know. If you want to come down to Levittown sometime I'll have a nice room."

"Thank you Henry. But I'm sure there will be plenty of girls in your new school who would gladly drive around in your car with you."

Henry paused, looking at her for a long moment.

"Come on Kreiser," Dearborn said.

Henry left with Dearborn.

On his last day at Milton Hershey, Henry finished packing his boxes. Then he put on his aviator sunglasses and tousled his hair. He slipped an earring in his ear, poking through the layer of skin that had healed from the piercing months earlier. He wandered through the house and outside and then went up to the pasture to look at the cows. He saw McGlinchy over at the barn. When McGlinchy saw Henry, he shook his head and gave Henry the middle finger. Henry returned the favor double time, bringing both middle fingers up to the sky and mouthing the words "Fuck you."

CHAPTER 7

From the off-ramp of the Pennsylvania Turnpike, which passed over an industrial complex, Henry saw Levittown both close up and sprawling into the distance. Next to the highway was a rundown apartment complex where a black family gathered around a card table in a coned-off parking spot under a laundry line. Across the road from the apartment complex was a one-story home where a half-dozen long-haired white kids stared into the motor of an old car up on blocks.

Kate slammed on the brakes suddenly when they reached the Mill Creek Parkway. Two cars raced down the wrong side of the road, just in front of Kate's bumper. "What assholes," she said.

Henry watched the cars rip past, kicking up dust. It was a big sixties muscle car versus a late-model import. The muscle car had the lead but then lost it around a curve to the smaller, more agile one.

"Whoa!" Henry watched out the back window as Kate turned onto the parkway.

Everybody attended the welcome-home dinner for Henry and Byron that evening.

"Hey, all," Henry said, taking a bite of chocolate cake after dinner. They all turned to him. "I want to just say, I'm glad we're all back together again. I feel like ..." Henry paused and looked down.

"What, Henry?" Teddy asked.

"I feel like ..." He got choked up. "I feel like this is a whole new beginning for me, and I thank you all for being ..."

"Go 'head. Let it go," Kate said. She looked at Chuck, who looked at Liz, who looked at Teddy, and they all got a little misty, except for Byron. Kate moved her chair closer and put her arm over Henry's shoulder. "You're going to be a good kid, right? Do well in school and work hard?"

"Am I going to be a good kid? I'm going to be the best kid in all of Levittown. You'll be so happy you took me out of Milton Hershey!"

"Good," Byron said. "You better be."

After dessert they sat around the house, watching TV in the living room and playing Trivial Pursuit in the dining room.

"You want to play, Henry?" Kate asked.

"Nah," Henry said. "Gonna watch TV."

He watched "Facts of Life" for a bit then grew bored and went outside. Teddy got up, motioned for Chuck to come along then followed Henry outside.

Outside, Teddy and Chuck confronted Henry, where he was sitting on the porch railing. "No fuck-ups, right?" Teddy asked.

"What?"

"I said, no fuck-ups, right?"

"Byron told us about your shit at Hershey," Chuck said. "Stealing and smoking."

"Oh, that? Yeah, I messed up. I'm starting with a clean slate here, though. I'm gonna be real good."

Teddy and Chuck looked at each other. "Okay," Teddy said. "Just don't bullshit us."

"No. No. Of course not."

A few days later, while Henry was watching TV, somebody honked a car horn several times. He went to the front window. Byron was there, standing next to a Subaru Brat, a tan, sporty car with a bed like a pickup truck.

Henry ran out and walked around it as Byron stood back. "How fast does it go?" Henry asked.

"It's not a race car."

"No, but how fast? Zero to sixty."

"That's why you're not going to drive it—ever."

"What? Why?" Henry asked.

"Because you're not responsible," Byron said, getting into the driver's seat.

"Come on. Don't be like that. Let me drive it."

"You don't have a driver's license anyway. Get in."

"I'll have one soon!" Henry jumped in. "And I'll show you how to race it."

That weekend Byron and Henry went out on the town in the Subaru. Night had fallen on the Fairless Hills Shopping Center—two strips of one-story shops. Suburban apartment complexes and tract housing developments surrounded it. V&S Pizza was there. So were a Pathmark, Bucks County Bank, and Po' Folks Restaurant. All were closed for the night. Next to the Fashion Bug, though, was Neon Nights, a club with flashing lights in the windows. Byron and Henry cruised in circles around the buildings of the shopping center. Henry watched the other cars pass by, amazed at how loud they played their music. A sporty red Pontiac Fiero played rap with heavy beats. A muscle car played rock and roll. Byron and Henry parked and approached Neon Nights. Byron was wearing purple spandex shorts and a stringy tank top while Henry had jeans and a black T-shirt. Kids packed in the entrance. Club boys were dressed with puffy pants full of pleats—hair was buzzed on sides and on top, real high. Girls had short ruffle skirts and big hair blown up in front.

Byron grabbed Henry's glasses from his face. "If you can't pick up a chick here," he told Henry, handing the glasses back to him, "then you can't pick up a chick."

"Unless you just want to have fun and don't want to pick up a chick." Henry put his glasses back on.

Inside the club, music thumped the chest. White kids, black kids, and a handful of Puerto Ricans all watched an empty dance floor.

"Check her out," Henry said, pointing at a black girl who was the first one on the dance floor. She had some moves. A few boys followed with some muted dance moves. Then, when several more girls started dancing with several guys, the music changed. The tempo picked up causing even more to go on the dance floor. Henry watched, transfixed, as a girl and guy danced around each other for several moments before spinning off to go dance with others.

On the next song, a solid electronic beat shook Henry—to the point he could no longer stay still. He moved to the edge of the dance floor and twirled his hands in front and threw a fist toward the sky. He twirled his hands together again and threw his other fist to the sky. He closed his eyes and hopped as he moved. When Byron saw a few of the girls laughing at Henry he went onto the dance floor and grabbed Henry's arm to stop him.

Henry yanked his arm out of Byron's hand. "Why'd you do that?"

Byron motioned for Henry to come join him off to the side. "Talk to me."

"What?"

"Just come over here and talk to me. Just pretend like we're talking." Byron leaned forward. "What are you doing?"

"What?" Henry asked defensively.

"That stupid dance."

"That's what we used to do at the Milt. Remember? I invented that."

"Well, it might have worked there but not here."

"People liked it," Henry said. "So leave me alone."

"People were laughing *at* you, Henry. Not *with* you. I hate to break it to you, but it was all a joke there, and it's a joke here. Sit down and watch me bust the groove."

Henry went over to bleacher-style seating and climbed to the top. He sat down.

After a while, the music tempo doubled. The beats now slammed the air and shook the walls of the club. The boys and girls responded. The party picked up, and the dance floor filled. Henry watched as Byron threw himself in the middle, dancing in a circle and using his elbows to push other dancers out of the middle. His dance moves, which bore a striking resemblance to his basketball moves, impressed several other dancers. They began to clap and backed up to open a circle around Byron. Then a black boy entered. Byron turned to the boy and began dancing as if he was running. He threw a leg out every fourth beat. He punched his fist in the air. The other boy responded by doing the same dance. They danced face to face, running in place. The girls and boys watching cheered them on while Henry laughed hysterically and started clapping for Byron.

When the song finished, the circle broke and all started dancing to the next song. Henry watched as two girls approached Byron. Then an icy cloud of fog flooded the dance floor from a machine on the ceiling, concealing his view. Henry climbed down from the bleacher seating and walked around in the fog, watching kids dance. Several songs started and finished as he walked around. He saw a pack of girls he wanted to approach but instead he stopped and leaned on a nearby wall to watch them. Behind them, on another set of bleacher seating Henry spotted Byron. He was making out with a girl—a black-haired Latin girl.

Later, after the club closed, Henry found himself in the back of the Subaru Brat, under the stars with a girl, while Byron was in the front with the girl he was kissing earlier. They were parked at Lake Caroline, a man-made lake across from the shopping center. Henry glanced over at the girl next to him, who sat there awkwardly and seemed unapproachable to Henry. Her black hair was pulled back tightly from her face and hoop earrings dangled against her cheeks. Her mini-skirt was snug and short and required her to keep her legs turned to the side to prevent Henry from spying into her private life. Henry struggled to come up with the right words to penetrate her cold silence. He looked to the front and saw Byron making out with her friend.

"Did you see that dance I did in there?" he asked, finally breaking the silence.

"No," she said, without engaging Henry with the slightest courtesy.

"I invented it one time at Milton Hershey, this

boarding school I used to go to. And everybody was doing it. So ..."

She nodded and then turned and knocked on the window to the front. When Byron opened it, she motioned to her friend in the front seat. "Let's go," she said.

That ended Byron's and Henry's first foray into brotherly girl-chasing. On their way home, after dropping off the girls, Byron stopped at a traffic light and turned to Henry. "Listen. Do you want me to teach you how to mac these chicks?"

"I know how."

"Then why didn't you move on that girl?"

"I was waiting for the right opportunity, man."

"No, you missed the opportunity, *man*."

"Ah, come on. I was just being easy on her. I could have..."

Byron laughed as the light turned green and he took off.

The following week Henry spotted Byron sunbathing in the backyard so joined him—sitting down in a lawn chair and leaning back. "Hey, man," Henry said.

"What's up, nut?"

"Yo, you had some rhymes with that girl the other night, didn't you?"

"Damn straight."

"What did you say? I mean ... what, like, did you ..."

Byron sat up and looked at him. "Oh, so you *do* want me to teach you now?"

Henry shrugged. "Yeah, I guess. I mean, no. Yes."

"But the other day you said you already know how to do it."

"I mean, I do. But I just want to know what you ... like, how you do it. So we can compare notes."

Byron leaned back in his chair, closed his eyes and turned his face to the sun. "Listen. I would just give it up, Henry."

"What?"

"I've been watching you for years, and I used to think you would grow up and be more like me—like the athletic type that macs chicks. But you didn't. Instead, I've seen you struggle to be somebody you're not."

"I don't do that!"

"But that's what you don't understand," Byron insisted, looking at Henry now, while shielding his own eyes from the sun. "You're a smart kid. You look like a smart kid. So why don't you just become that kid? The smart kid."

"Why do you have ... why do you have to say that?"

"It's a compliment, man. You should thank me."

"I'm not *the smart kid*!"

"You asked, and I'm telling you what you can do."

Henry gave Byron the middle finger, walked in the house, and slammed the door.

"And you gotta be less sensitive!" Byron yelled.

A couple weeks later Henry burst out the doors of the Department of Motor Vehicles, behind the Neshaminy Mall in Langhorne. Kate trailed behind. Henry kneeled and punched the ground. "Yes! I can finally freakin' drive."

Kate looked at a notepad as Henry drove her car—a Buick sedan. "I put some thought into when you can use my car," she said. "I want you to use it only at specific times. I don't need you riding around any time you want."

"Okay. Sure."

"Monday and Tuesday evenings, between seven and ten, so you get practice driving when it's dark, and Saturday afternoons from noon to five."

"That's it?"

"That's all you need."

"What about when I go out on Friday or Saturday night?" Henry stopped the car at a traffic light.

"Nope," she said.

"No?"

"No. I don't want you driving it around when you go partying."

Henry cruised in Byron's Subaru Brat one day through the Fairless Hills Shopping Center. He drove slowly past the front of Pathmark, stopping for shoppers with loaded carts of groceries. In front of the V&S Pizza he locked eyes with a young man wearing a baseball cap and basketball shorts. Henry slumped back in his seat a bit more, brought his hand to the top of the steering wheel and drove around the corner of the building at the end of the shopping center. He was about to hit the gas but instead hit the brakes hard. A girl with dark, curly hair darted in front of the Brat, not even realizing she almost got hit. She searched through her purse as she crossed the side lot of the shopping center. She pushed her curls back, and Henry glimpsed an olive complexion. He watched her for a second and began following her—just ten or twenty yards behind. She stopped so he stopped. She pulled out a compact, brought her lips close the mirror and applied lipstick. After she walked a bit more she arrived at her destination—a Fotomat booth in the middle of the empty parking lot. She entered the side door and opened the blinds. As he pulled up to it and looked inside, she placed an 'OPEN' sign in the window. She finally became aware of Henry's presence, so she opened the window. But, with the loss of anonymity Henry grew nervous. "Can I help you, sir?" She had a slight accent that Henry didn't recognize.

Henry searched for the handle to roll down the window but couldn't find it. She watched him as he searched. After a few seconds, he opened the door and popped his head out of the car. "I was just—ahhh!" The car lurched forward, so he jumped back in and slammed the brakes. He turned the motor off, pulled up the emergency brake, and popped his head back out. "Did you say something?"

She laughed. "I asked, can I help you, sir?"

"Oh. No." He got back in the driver's seat and started the car, then pulled slowly away keeping his eyes on her.

She shrugged at him.

That Saturday night Henry came running down the steps to the living room where Byron was watching TV.

"Let's go to Neon Nights," Henry said.

"Nah. Gonna hang with my girl."

"Come on!" Henry grabbed the remote control from the coffee table and flicked over to another channel.

Byron grabbed it back and changed the channel back. "Go yourself," he said.

"No."

"You afraid?" Byron asked, looking in Henry's eyes.

"No. I'm not afraid."

"But it would be easier to mac the chicks if you have a wing man, right?"

Henry flopped back and put his feet up on the coffee table. "Yeah. I guess it would."

When Byron and Henry entered Neon Nights, the beats were already pounding the air. They grabbed two Cokes, stood in the corner next to the dance floor, and watched the crowd. The beats instantly put their trance on Henry. Before he even had two sips, Henry put his Coke down on the bar. "Watch this," he said, moving toward the dance floor.

Byron grabbed his arm. "What are you doing?"

"I'm gonna dance."

"Don't go doing that weird shit, man. You'll never mac the chicks with that."

Henry pulled his arm away and shuffled to the beat over to the dance floor. Byron watched as Henry once again started twirling and throwing his fists to the sky. Byron threw his face in his hands. "Not again," he said to himself.

People paid little attention to Henry so he had to hold elbows wide to make space. A second later, when the beat tempo increased, Henry was transformed—his funny twirl and punch slowly became a stomp and jump. His face was fierce. His moves were not only unconventional; they were off-the-charts strange. Then his stomp and jump turned into a unique form of Running Man. His feet hit the floor on every beat as he began running in place. He even worked in a move to poke his glasses back on his nose before they fell off. And suddenly, the crowd grew aware of Henry, parted and formed a circle around him. Byron laughed, almost choked on a piece of ice, and then put his coke down. He shoved his way through the crowd to watch Henry in action. He clapped and laughed as Henry drew the attention of everybody in the room.

Go white boy, go white boy, go white boy, go!
Go white boy, go white boy, go white boy, go!

Henry danced the Running Man unchallenged, so Byron jumped in. He and Henry danced off, running in place. Byron had solid, fluid moves—he pumped his fist to the sky, he slapped the butt then rode the horse. And the crowds cheered for him. But Henry took the unconventional approach. He worked in his signature twirls and fist throws, and some stomp and jump. Then, out of nowhere, as he was slapping the butt, he threw in two pelvis thrusts. He slapped the butt and again threw in two pelvis thrusts. And the crowd went crazy. They laughed and cheered again.

When they finished, Henry and Byron high-fived each other. The crowds converged to fill the circle the Kreisers left behind. Henry had sweat on his brow and his ears rang with euphoria. He smiled as he hadn't in a long time and moved with a swagger. He felt all eyes were on him so he glanced around, making eye contact with those whose gaze he found. He nodded and smiled proudly to them. As he searched the room for more people to connect with, he noticed a girl approaching him. It was the Fotomat girl with the long black curls. She danced in front of him, so he started dancing again. He moved toward her quickly while he danced. But then her friend arrived and grabbed her arm. The girls walked away, leaving Henry standing alone. From the edge of the dance floor Byron had seen Henry's attempt and ultimate failure.

Byron drove home. "Something you're finally good at," he said to Henry, whose swagger from the dance floor even possessed his seated posture. He had a foot up on the dashboard and his hands clasped behind his head.

"Damn straight," Henry said. "I think I'm better than you."

"Settle down, tough guy. You gotta drop the weird shit first."

"I ain't gotta drop nothing. They liked my style."

Byron shrugged. "Some did, but you still didn't get the chick."

In early-August Byron packed his clothes in a suitcase.

Henry sat nearby. "Since you can't have a car on campus, I was thinking—"

"No. Don't even think about it. The car is going to sit here with its doors locked."

"Come on, man!" Henry grabbed a shirt and threw it in Byron's suitcase.

"No—you'll wreck the thing."

"No. I promise I won't."

"I said no." Byron pulled out the shirt that Henry had thrown in and refolded it.

"How am I supposed to pick up chicks if I can't drive?"

Byron shook his head.

"You want me to take the bus? Walk to Neon Nights? I'll be stuck here."

"I paid a lot of money for that car."

"I told you. I'll take good care of it."

Byron finished packing his suitcase and closed it. "Why do you have to make me feel sorry for you all the time?"

Henry smiled. "Nothing will happen. Promise."

A couple weeks later, Henry woke up on Sunday morning on the couch. MTV was still on from the night before so he sat up and watched. A game show, 'Remote Control', was on.

Kate, wearing a dress, came out of her room. "You coming to church?"

"Nah." Henry stayed focused on the TV.

"Where'd you go last night?"

"Huh?"

"Will you pay attention to me? I asked, where'd you go last night?"

"Oh," he straightened up on the couch and pushed the blanket aside. "Just went down to Neon Nights."

"To the dance club?"

"Yeah."

"Yeah, well, you're supposed to ask when you take the car."

"I am!?" he asked, defensively. "You gave me instructions on when I can use your car and I have not used your car at all. So what difference does it make?"

"Don't play stupid, and don't try to change the subject. I told you before—this isn't anything goes. You should have asked me—even if it was Byron's car."

"Okay. Sorry." Henry went back to watching TV.

Kate stood there for a long time. She shuffled. She watched Henry watch the TV then threw her purse down on the couch. "Don't make light of what I tell you."

"Okay. I'm sorry."

Jack came out of the bedroom wearing a suit. He shook his head in dismay at Henry. Kate grabbed her purse and walked out with Jack.

Henry watched dance songs and rocks songs, and then *Yo MTV Raps* came on. He watched some videos then got up and danced a bit. A black singer with ridiculously baggy pants and a tall flat-top haircut came on. He called himself Hammer. As Hammer danced, Henry became intrigued. The song was one that he and Byron had danced to several times at Neon Nights. He sat down to watch Hammer. Hammer rapped about being strong like a lion—about being the master. Henry watched Hammer's feet—he couldn't believe Hammer's feet. When the chorus came on—"Turn this mutha out"—Henry got up and watched the screen closely. He began moving his own feet trying to emulate Hammer. He fumbled at first then, slowly, he felt the rhythm and found the beat.

As Henry stomped and slid, Hammer's Running Man became another dance altogether—unrecognizable and strange by all measures. Henry followed step for step and his Running Man also became a different dance. He imagined himself dancing face to face with Hammer. His feet stomped to the floor. He threw a leg, slid to the right, hopped on the horse and rode it away. Henry laughed to himself as the song finished and the VJ came back on the screen. He ran upstairs. He whipped his glasses off his face and looked closely in the mirror at the vein pulsing on his temple.

That week Kate gave Henry sixty dollars to buy some clothes for school, so he went to the mall.

At Merry Go Round, he bought a shiny, ornate shirt.

At the Wall he bought MC Hammer's cassette tape.

At the Hair Cuttery, Henry leaned back in the chair. He put his head back in the sink. A young lady put shampoo in his hair and massaged his scalp.

"I want something mac," he said, with his eyes closed. "Know what I mean?"

"No" she said.

He opened his eyes, and her breasts were there right in front of him. He heard the fabric of her shirt rub against the fabric of her bra. He closed his eyes and smelled her perfume. "First a perm," he said. "Then a flat-top."

After she finished shampooing and wrapped a towel around his shoulders, Henry reached in his pocket and pulled out a picture. He showed her MC Hammer on a cassette cover.

She laughed.

When done, Henry put on his glasses to examine his new hairstyle in the mirror. The girl stood behind him. "You like it?" she asked.

His curly flat-top was tall and made his head look long and thin. "I love it!"

When Henry returned to Neon Nights on Saturday he had a whole new look. His ornate shirt glimmered in the flashing lights. Catching a glimpse of himself in the mirror, he paused and examined his flat-topped curls.

"Sir," the barmaid said.

Henry touched the top of his hair, not hearing her.

"Sir," she said again.

"Oh. I was just ... What?"

"I asked if I could get you something."

"Coke is good."

As the party and beats took on a quickened tempo, Henry's excitement grew. Once the dance floor had a half dozen people on it he stepped on to join them. He worked his unconventional dance style then quickly turned it into the Running Man. But it was an even wilder Running Man—the one he learned from Hammer. He went face to face with a black kid—slapping, pumping and twirling his hands. He threw his signature pelvis thrust and the crowd cheered him on.

After a long session on the floor, Henry took a break and leaned on the bar to catch his breath. And that's when he saw her again—the Fotomat girl—on the dance floor. She saw him, too, at the same moment. He stepped back on the floor and danced in front of her. She turned to him and moved with him. She examined him from top to bottom, his pants, his shirt, and his hair. She leaned toward him with interest. But when he clumsily poked his glasses back she stopped suddenly and walked away. Henry froze and had difficulty finding the beat, so he stopped and left the dance floor.

After getting a Coke, he spotted her near the bar with a bunch of friends, mostly Latin guys and girls. Henry slid along the bar, sneaking up next to them. Some of the guys soon left for the dance floor, leaving just the Fotomat girl and her friend standing there next to him. Henry moved even closer and tried to make eye contact. Her friend turned away from Henry, and at the same moment, when he thought the Fotomat girl was about to walk away also, she approached him.

"What's up?" he said, extending his hand to her.

She looked at it. "Listen. I'm not interested. Okay?"

Henry froze and looked down at his Coke as she walked away. Henry watched the ice bobbing in his Coke for several minutes then sipped it until it was gone.

"Can I get you another one?" the barmaid asked.

Henry looked at her without saying anything then turned his head down in embarrassment.

A new song with a heavy beat started playing. As he was standing there, wallowing in embarrassment, the beat reached him. It shook his glass and jingled the ice. It penetrated his wallowing. He turned to the dance floor and saw the crowd going wild. Their joy suddenly angered him. He ran to the dance floor and grabbed the arm of a small white kid wearing overalls.

"That's not how you do it, weirdo," Henry said.

"What?" The kid was startled.

"Nothing." Henry shook his head. He started dancing. In one swift movement, he yanked his glasses from his face and put them in his pocket. First he danced the jump-and-pump and then the twirl-and-throw. Then, the Running Man came alive. He danced face to face with several people, but he did so aggressively. He got in their faces and pumped his fist. He twirled and hopped. And each time he went face to face, a circle started to form. But before the crowd could encircle him, he pulled away and moved on to a new person. Tension rose around Henry. A Latin boy in extraordinarily baggy pants stopped dancing and brought his girlfriend's attention to Henry.

Once Henry felt the tension rise to an almost explosive level, he turned inward. He stopped going head to head with others and then danced with himself. He kept his eyes closed and held his arms high. For the next hour, he danced that way. Neon Nights was crowded that night, but Henry was alone. He threw in one pelvis thrust after the next. He was slopped in sweat. When the lights came on, Henry walked for the door, ramming his shoulder into anybody that was in his way.

Out front, a blond long-haired kid parked his pristinely restored sixties Mustang and approached the front of the club, yelling something angrily.

Henry, exiting the club at that moment, jumped back and dodged to the side. The hair on the back of his neck stood up, as he clenched his fist, anticipating a fight. Looking out into the parking lot, he saw two other long-haired kids get out of the Mustang and begin to follow their friend toward the club entrance.

"Fuck him up, Rick!" one of them called to the first kid. "I.C. Posse is here!"

"That's right," Rick said, "I'm gonna fuck him up." Rick ran forward aggressively, and Henry nearly fell over as he prepared for the attack. But Rick passed Henry at the last moment and ran right up to a burly, short-haired kid who was leaning on a concrete barrier. "What you got Stanley?" Rick got in the burly kid's face.

"I'll tell you what I got," Stanley said. He stepped forward and slapped Rick across the side of the head with his thick and heavy hand. He then cocked back and punched Rick in the face. As Rick fell, Stanley grabbed his long hair and yanked his head toward the ground. The other two long-haired kids who had emerged from the Mustang quickly turned around and got back in it – one in the backseat and one in the passenger seat. Walking away from Rick, who was picking himself off the ground, Stanley sauntered up to the Mustang and looked inside.

"What's the I.C. Posse got now?" Stanley asked.

The two kids stared ahead, avoiding eye contact.

Henry gathered himself and was pleasantly surprised he was not the one Rick was going after. A group of guys had seen Henry's little freak out and were laughing. He gave them the middle finger and walked over to the Subaru when he saw Stanley getting into a nearby sports car. He glanced over at Henry.

"What up," Henry said.

Stanley got in his car and sped away.

Henry drove home on the Mill Creek Parkway. When he stopped at a traffic light, another car pulled alongside his. It was Rick and his two friends in the Mustang. The one in the passenger seat flicked a cigarette butt out the window, looked over at Henry, and began laughing. "Look at that freakin' sissy car, man," he said to his friends. "It's like a car but like a pickup truck."

Henry heard them laughing. He looked over at them, smiled, and raised his hand as if he was going to wave. But instead of waving, he turned his hand around, gave them the middle finger, then drove quickly away.

When Henry pulled in front of his house and turned off the lights, another car pulled up behind him and turned off its lights. Henry turned off his car and heard the motor of the other car—a throaty muscle-car sound. He looked in the rearview mirror and saw the white stripe of the Mustang. Curious and somewhat scared he waited in the car and watched in his rearview mirror. Then he heard several hoots and saw them high-five each other and get out of the car. Henry went to open his door but then froze. They arrived on either side of the Brat.

"It really is a sissy car." Rick reached over and grabbed a windshield wiper. He ripped it up and broke it back; then he yanked it from the car.

"Get out," another one said.

Henry got out and faced them.

"Do you know who you just gave the middle finger to?"

"You?" Henry asked.

"Ha ha. The I.C. Posse. How about that?" He pointed in Henry's face. "And when you wrong one of us you deal with all of us."

While Rick was talking, one of the other two was mimicking Henry's every move. When Henry moved his arm so did he. When Henry shifted he shifted too. Henry noticed and glanced at him, trying to figure out what he was doing. But he also realized something else peculiar at that moment—they were all wearing flannel shirts and had the left sleeve rolled up to the elbow and right sleeve down all the way and buttoned.

"Why'd you do it?" Rick asked.

"I don't know," Henry shrugged. "I just pulled up my hand and that's all."

"Say you're sorry."

Henry said nothing.

"I said, say you're sorry," Rick kicked toward Henry. "You fuckin' weirdo with a weird fuckin' car and weirder fuckin' hair!"

Henry shifted quickly on his feet, thinking he was about to fight. "Not sorry," he blurted.

"What did you say?" Rick smacked Henry across the face with the wiper. His glasses slid down on his face. "You four-eyed freak!"

Henry snapped. In one quick movement he whipped the glasses from his face and slipped them in his pocket.

"*What?*" He leaped at Rick and grabbed the windshield wiper. "What the fuck did you say?" Henry swung the wiper at Rick. Then he swung it at the others. He jabbed at them like it was a sword.

"Yo, spaz. We were just saying you shouldn't do that," Rick said.

"Well, you know what? I used to fuckin' dress like you. But I grew the fuck up. Pond people—that's what you are. And I'll fuck you the fuck up."

The one that was mimicking Henry's movements now stepped forward and reached out to grab Henry, but Henry jabbed the windshield wiper at him. Then he smacked it on top of his own head and threw it to the ground. "You want to fuck with me?"

A light went on in Henry's house. All four of them looked over at the house for a moment.

"Let's go," Rick said.

"Shouldn't we fuck him up," one of the other guys asked.

"Oh we will. You wrong I.C. Posse and you get what's coming to you." They walked off. "He hit himself with the windshield wiper... what the fuck was that?" They all laughed as they got back in the Mustang.

As Rick pulled the car away he screeched the tires.

Henry watched them leave and then picked up the windshield wiper and threw it in the bed of the Brat.

Inside, Kate was waiting, sitting in the living room in her robe with the TV on. "Hey. What was going on out there?"

"Out where?"

"Outside. I heard another car and some people."

"Oh, that?" Henry asked.

"Yes. That."

"Just some people passing by, that's all."

"But you were talking to them."

"Me?" he asked, with a contrived surprised look.

"Henry! Stop playing dumb."

"What are you watching?" He looked at the TV.

"What does it look like?" she asked.

"The news?"

"How did you guess? Now sit down."

"I think I'm gonna go to bed actually." He started toward the steps.

"Sit down for moment, please. I want to talk to you about some things."

"I'll stand."

"Henry." She sighed and turned off the television. "I want to be as clear as day when I tell you this. You start school next week, and I want you to do well. This staying-out-late business is not going to work."

"Well, you know what I was thinking? I might not even go back to school," he said defiantly. "I think I just might find a job so I can get my own place." He ran up the stairs.

She was stunned to silence.

In his room, he undressed down to his underwear and looked at himself in the mirror. Then he hit the floor and started doing push-ups aggressively. And he stood again in front of the mirror and flexed and punched. His glasses slid down his nose—which was slippery from sweat. He did more push-ups, and his glasses slid off his face and fell on the floor. He put them back on, got up, and punched at the mirror more. Then, in the passion of the punch, his glasses completely fell off his face and fell to the floor. He huffed, agitated, and looked at them on the floor. One arm of his glasses was bent. He shook his head in anger, and in a sudden fury, he stamped his glasses repeatedly. He broke them to bits.

In the morning, Henry smelled bacon and eggs. Morning hunger was insatiable. He got dressed, but when he was about to go downstairs, he stopped. He heard Kate talking, as well as several others. He sat on his bed for a while. Then the smell reached his nose again so he went down.

When he got downstairs, he saw in his blurred vision that several people were sitting around the dining room table. They stopped talking as Henry approached. He moped into the room and was able to see who was there: Byron, Chuck and Veronica, Teddy, Liz, Kate, and Jack.

They had plates full of eggs and bacon and French toast. Henry took an empty seat. He filled his plate with eggs and bacon and started eating.

Chuck drank his orange juice to the bottom and put his glass down. "Quitting school is not an option, Henry."

Henry looked at him and then at Kate.

"It would be stupid," Byron said. "That would make you a dumb-ass."

"You want to spend your life digging ditches?" Teddy asked.

Henry turned to Liz. "You didn't finish high school, did you, Liz?"

"No. But I got my GED. And I wish I'd finished."

"But you have a decent job?"

She shrugged in reluctant agreement. "Yeah."

"See? She has a good job. So why can't I start working? I'm sixteen!"

"Exactly. Because you *are* sixteen." Kate said. "And because you don't have to, Henry. I'm willing to support you."

"And I really appreciate that, but I want to start supporting myself."

"Why would you want to do that?" Chuck asked.

"You all support yourselves. I wanna do the same. I want a car. I want a house. It's not fair I'm the only one who's not allowed to..."

"You're the youngest," Liz said. "It's our job to look out for you."

"Hey!" Henry slammed his fork down. "I want to be independent. Okay?" He stood to leave. "Okay?"

"Mom and Dad would have never, ever wanted you to quit school, Henry, and you know it." Kate said.

Henry sat back down. He nodded. "They wouldn't have, would they?"

"No," she said.

Henry put some more French toast on his plate and began eating again. Kate's words echoed in his mind: *Mom and Dad would have never, ever wanted you to quit school.* He finished his French toast. "Okay. I'll do it." He reached into his pocket and pulled out his broken glasses. "But I need somebody to buy me contact lenses so I can see the chalkboard. I don't want to wear glasses anymore."

"Deal!" Byron jumped up and slapped him on the back.

After the others left the house, Kate went into the kitchen to do the dishes. Henry remained at the table alone. Looking around the room, still with blurred vision, he noticed something in the middle of the table reflecting the Sunday morning light. He reached across and picked it up—a large knife. He ran his finger on the sharp edge and touched the point. Then he slipped it up his sleeve and went out to the car.

He searched below the driver's seat and found a spot to stash it. Then, he sat in the car, as if driving, and reached down to grab the knife. *He pulled it out quickly as though he was defending himself* – as if somebody was at the window. After stashing the knife again, he grabbed the broken windshield wiper from the truck bed and tried to reattach it where it had broken off, but it was beyond repair. He stood still, thinking for a moment and then laid the broken wiper in the crevice between the hood and the windshield.

CHAPTER 8

On the first day of school, buses ruled the road. Henry drove the Subaru slouched down and pumped up the MC Hammer. He drove fast and screeched the tires at every chance. On the longer stretches, he sped beyond the limit and checked his coif in the rearview mirror. When he passed a bus, squealing his tires, a fat kid stuck his head out the bus window and laughed and pointed. Henry smiled and brought his hand up as if to wave but then gave him the middle finger.

In front of Truman High School, a wide, one-story tan brick building, he cruised slowly and leaned back. The school sign read, "Welcome The Class of 1988". Cars were lined up in both directions. The small, sporty cars in reds and yellows played rap and dance, while the classic muscle cars in blues and blacks played heavy metal and classic rock. Most of them had music much louder than Henry's, with systems that shook his windows with bass. He parked along the road, half in a drainage ditch. While walking in, he saw the white-striped Mustang parked nearby.

When he got to the front of the building, he saw a familiar face near each of the two main entrances. At one entrance was Stanley, the big no-neck kid who had gotten in the fight in front of Neon Nights. Around him was a crowd of athletes in their varsity jackets, pretty high-hair girls, and other muscle kids. There were blacks and whites. At the other entrance, under a cloud of cigarette smoke, was Rick, the blond-haired guy that had broken off Henry's windshield wiper. Also in that area were other long-haired kids in flannel shirts smoking cigarettes—rocker types that were mostly white. A handful of them, including Rick, were wearing their flannels with one sleeve rolled up and one down as Henry witnessed on Rick and his friends a few nights prior.

Henry walked directly toward the main entrance, where the varsity types were, and stopped near Stanley. He watched and listened, as if he was suddenly a part of their crowd. A black kid in a varsity jacket started bobbing and weaving around Stanley playfully. "Come on, Stanley. You big, but you slow, motherfucker."

Henry laughed at the antics for a moment, but Stanley shot him a glance so Henry turned away, trying to act as if he wasn't watching. The boxing kid continued to bounce around Stanley, throwing slaps toward his head. Henry started to watch again, more cautiously this time. Stanley was calm and even amused at first, but then one of the slaps connected with the side of his head—and everything changed. Stanley's eyes flashed angry. He lunged forward and, with both arms, yanked the black kid in and clamped his arms around him. He picked him up above his head causing the other varsity kids to gather around and erupt in laughter.

Henry jumped backward to get out of the way and started laughing. "Aw, shit. He got you, motherfucker!"

Everybody stopped suddenly and looked at Henry, who was clutching his crotch in his fist and pointing. Henry stopped pointing and released his crotch. There was a long silence as Stanley put the black kid down. Henry touched his hair nervously. "I gotta go, guys. Just need to go in and find out what class I'm in." He walked into the entrance with a self-conscious gait—first taking steps he felt were too small, tripping a little to readjust his pace, then taking steps he felt were too big.

"Who the hell is that kid?" the black kid asked Stanley.

"I don't know. Some new freak, I guess. I saw him outside Neon Nights the other night. But I think he had glasses then."

Henry kept quiet and out of way as he went through

his classes that day. When he walked into chemistry class, he saw Stanley so sat down next to him.

"Henry Kreiser." Henry extended his hand.

Stanley looked at Henry's hand and then looked away.

Midway through the class, the teacher wrote something on the board as the class chattered.

"Potato salad," Stanley said.

Everybody looked around to see who Stanley was talking to. He pointed to Henry's hair.

"He's talking to you," a girl next to Henry told him.

"Potato salad?" Henry asked Stanley. "Hungry?"

Stanley shook his head. "Your hair looks like potato salad. Did you get a perm?" Everybody laughed.

"Well, you got a potato head," Henry said. "In fact, you actually look like Mr. Potato Head." The others laughed hysterically.

"Don't gimme no lip, dude. I'll mash you into mashed potatoes."

At the end of the first day of school, Henry searched the empty hallways. Near the gymnasium he found what he was looking for—the weight room. Stanley was there, as were two of the varsity football guys—one stocky with brown hair and the other tall and thin. The second Henry walked through the door, the two friends stopped what they were doing and stared at him. He circled around a rack of dumbbells and over to a bench press. Stanley was bench-pressing a barbell with three big plates on either side. Henry put one big plate on each side of his and lay on the bench. He started immediately with a huge grunt and pushed the bar to the ceiling. He arched his back. The bar tipped a little, so he lifted his foot to regain balance.

Stanley finished and sat up to watch Henry. "Check this guy out," he said to the others.

Henry lowered the weight down to his chest quickly and pushed it up hard and fast while holding his breath. And again he let it drop to his chest. But when he went to push it back up the second time, it didn't move. He pushed and huffed but was stuck. He had been holding his breath and let it out in one huge exhale.

Stanley ran over to Henry, lifted the barbell off Henry's chest and put it on the rack. "Football team has the weight room from three to four," Stanley told him.

Henry got up, embarrassed. He took the weights off the bar.

"And perms are for fags," Stanley continued. The other two laughed.

They watched Henry walk toward the door and Henry glanced back at them a couple times, wanting to come up with a retort. Finally, he stopped in the doorway, made a goofy face, and pretended to flex like a body builder. "Potatoes are for heads, potato head."

The other two football guys laughed so Stanley did too then stopped short. "That doesn't even make sense, potato salad head" Stanley said.

"Whatever." Henry left.

Henry walked into the guidance counselor's office about a week into the school year. Inside was a secretary's counter and beyond, an office. A man in a dark gray blazer and light gray slacks was standing in front of the secretary.

"Really, I need only one good, hard-working young man," the man said. "Just one. You writing this down?"

"Yes. I'm writing it down."

Henry overheard their conversation and was interested. He sat down in a chair and listened.

"He'll be working around heavy machinery. And he needs to be trustworthy, too. He should be able to lift boxes at least fifty pounds in weight. But I'll pay him well."

Henry stepped up to the counter. "Hi, sir. My name is Henry Kreiser. I'm the man for the job." Henry extended his hand. They shook hands.

"Well hello, young man. You work hard?"

"I do. I have a lot of experience. I worked in a barn."

"Can you lift heavy boxes?" The man reached out and put his hand around Henry's arm.

"I can. I'm thinner than I look."

"You're what?"

"I mean I'm stronger than I look. I'm thin but strong. I

used to carry bales of hay all day long."

"Are you trustworthy?"

Henry laughed. "Am I trustworthy? I'm the most trustworthy guy you'll ever meet."

"Done! I'm Clarence Penn, sole proprietor of Clarence J. Penn Bingo Supply. We sell bingo supplies to the world."

"Wait a second, young man," the secretary said. "Are you in the work program or college prep?"

"College prep, but I'd like to switch, please."

"Don't you want to talk to the guidance counselor first?"

"No thanks."

That afternoon, along the road in front of school, Henry spotted Stanley and the two football players he was lifting with the week prior, the stocky one and the tall one. They were standing across the street from the Mustang with the white stripe. Henry walked up to them.

"You know, I saw what happened," Henry said to Stanley.

"What are you talking about?" Stanley asked.

"The other night, in front of Neon Nights."

"You saw that?"

"Yup."

"See, guys?" Stanley said to the others. "Potato Salad here saw me whoop Rick's ass. I.C. Posse is nothing under these guns." Stanley slapped his own biceps.

"Yeah," Henry said. "Then I whooped his ass afterwards too. So ..." He kicked a clump of crabgrass.

"So... what?" the stocky guy asked. "What happened?"

"Nah. I flipped them the bird when I was driving home, and they followed me to my house. Then they broke the windshield wiper off my car so I flipped the fuck out."

"Really?" Stanley asked. "You?"

"Yeah, really. Next time you get in a fight, you should call me."

They all started laughing at Henry and turned away from him. He stood and kicked the clump of crabgrass for a long moment and then crossed the street to the Mustang, pulling out his keys. "Watch," Henry called over to them. He slowly walked the full length of the car, gouging a deep scratch with his keys. When he got to the end he looked back at it. He left a severe mark on the pristine paint job. Back across the street Stanley and the other two were walking quickly away.

"I gotta go, guys!" Henry called. "I got a job at the bingo supply factory so ..." They didn't hear him but he continued anyway. "So I'll just go, then. Catch up with you guys later!" He stood there glancing around to see if anybody had seen what he did. *Oh shit*, he thought. He ran off.

The following week, when Henry went into the weight room, Stanley was there by himself, bench-pressing. He was getting fatigued and his arms began to shake. He was about to set the barbell back on the rack when Henry ran to spot him.

"Come on, motherfucker. One more," Henry said, putting his hands on the bar. Stanley brought the weight down to his chest and then began to push it up again but reached a stopping point, just a couple inches off his chest, that he couldn't get it past. "Another, man – one more time." Henry said.

"I can't; that's it." Stanley tried to put the weight back, but Henry pushed the bar away from the rack.

"C'mon, just one more!" Henry yelled in his face.

Stanley started to laugh and lose control of the weight. He lowered it down again and struggled to push it back up, coming to a complete stop halfway up. After watching him struggle for a second, Henry helped him get the weight up on the rack.

"I know the football team has the weight room reserved at this time," Henry said, "but you won't tell on me if I lift now will you?"

"Nah," Stanley said, still on the bench recovering. "It's cool."

Henry went to another bench press and loaded some plates on the barbell. Stanley sat up and watched. "Where did you move from?"

"I'm from here originally, but I went to a boarding school out in central P.A."

"You a rich kid?"

"No. It was a school for kids from broken families." Henry began bench-pressing really fast and hard.

"Slow down, dude." Stanley stood above Henry to spot him. "Go slow to feel the muscles burn. That's how you get stronger."

Henry pushed until his muscles could do no more, and then Stanley forced him to do two more repetitions by blocking access to the rack. Henry's face turned red.

"Breathe out when you press up, and inhale when you bring it down!" Stanley helped him with the bar on the last rep. "You gotta calm down."

When Henry regained his energy, they both started curling dumbbells. "What happened to your family?" Stanley asked. "I mean, you had a broken family?"

"My parents died when I was younger."

Stanley stopped. "Really? Sorry to hear that, man."

Henry continued to curl. "It sucked. But you know, I'm okay."

"My mom died a couple of years ago too," Stanley said.

Henry put the dumbbells down. "I'm Henry Kreiser."

"Stanley Cassingham."

They shook hands.

"I want to get big like you," Henry said.

"Sorry to say this, Henry but I think maybe you just don't have the genes for it."

"Probably true, but I wanna get bigger."

"You'll have to really bust your ass. Have to go to muscle fatigue on every set. Slow lifting — that's how you do it."

"I can do that."

"And you'll probably need some help, still. Like supplements."

"What do you mean?"

"Like muscle fuel and amino acids. Then, my friend, you'll get big."

AMERICAN SPAZ

* * *

Henry fell into a routine. Monday, Wednesday, and Friday, he went to the weight room after school. Tuesday and Thursday, he only attended school for two hours before going to work at the bingo supply factory. He applied what he learned at the factory about lifting boxes to his weight-lifting routine: bend your knees and no sudden movements. And he applied what he learned from lifting weights with Stanley to his job at the factory: lift slowly, feel the muscles burn, and never work-out the same muscle group two days in a row.

One morning inside of school, Henry flashed a handful of cash to Stanley. It was mostly tens and fives but was an impressive bundle nonetheless. "I wanna buy some supplements, like you talked about."

"Well, let's go. Who needs school anyway?"

Henry paused. "Wait...do you mean now?"

"Yeah, let's skip class and go to the mall." Stanley headed for the door.

"Wait...I don't know. I have a test in math this afternoon."

"Come on," Stanley grabbed Henry by the arm. "We'll come back probably."

At the Oxford Valley Mall they found a vitamin store. Stanley knew the shelves pertaining to bodybuilding well. He pointed out the different supplements in big plastic bottles and little glass ones. "This is the one you want. Muscle Milk." It was a two gallon, round-shaped bottle. On the label was a man with unrealistically huge and shiny muscles.

"What does it do?" Henry asked.

"It restores the protein that gets broken down when you lift. You know how you feel pain the day after lifting?"

"Yeah."

"Well, that means your muscles are torn up, and you need to restore and rebuild with protein. The pain is a sign that something is not right. And you should do something about it."

They stopped at Arby's on Route 1 before driving back to school. As Henry drove, both he and Stanley ate roast beef sandwiches.

"You see," Stanley said with his mouth full, "beef is like pure protein. When your muscles are in pain, eat beef and drink Muscle Milk, and your pecs will explode."

Henry nodded. A long silence followed as they ate. When he finished, Henry wiped his mouth on his sleeve and glanced at Stanley. "I was thinking about something," Henry said.

"Yeah?"

"How did your Mom die?"

Stanley finished the last bite of his sandwich and took a drink of soda. "Cancer... and your mom and dad? How did they die?"

"Mom in a car accident and Dad of cancer."

They sat quietly again for several minutes. When they returned to school, they parked in the housing section to avoid getting caught. As they walked back Henry sipped his soda, and Stanley scooped coleslaw from a small cup.

"You're kind of cool, Kreiser. I thought you were a freak at first, but you're all right."

Henry laughed. "Thanks ... I think."

Stanley stopped suddenly and stared at something up the street. His eyes flit about nervously.

"What's going on?" Henry looked around and saw a police car coming toward them down the street.

"He's a truant officer," Stanley whispered. "We gotta run. On the count of three. One ... two ..."

"On the count of three, what?"

"Three! Run!" Stanley threw his coleslaw into the air, took off across the yard of the house they were in front of, and hurdled the privacy fence into the backyard.

Henry looked back and saw the police car stop and the officer get out quickly. Henry locked eyes with the officer for a second then dropped his soda and ran after Stanley. He took a running leap at the fence but slammed into it and fell to the ground. He saw the officer following across the lawn, so Henry scrambled back up to his feet and approached the fence again. Just when he thought he was busted, Stanley's hand came over the fence and yanked him over it. They ran across the lawn and jumped over the next fence. Henry again struggled and needed a hand from Stanley. From the second backyard, they watched through the fence at the next street and waited until the police car drove slowly past.

"You're not very agile, are you, Kreiser?"

"Yeah, I'm fast."

"No, agile. You gotta be able to stop quick, dodge, jump. You just slammed into the fence like a sack of potatoes."

Henry shrugged. "Whatever. I was just... I just got tripped up. There was this garden hose—"

"There was no garden hose." Stanley lurched forward as though he was going to hit Henry. Henry flinched severely to block the attack, and in doing so, he hit himself in the face with his arms. Stanley laughed. "See? You're not agile at all."

"Let's go back to school," Henry said.

In chemistry class that week, the students gathered around the countertops in the lab. Bunsen burners were lit, and beakers were full of water and other liquids. All the students wore goggles. Henry looked over at Stanley and made a weird face—he crossed his eyes and stuck out his tongue.

Stanley responded with a weirder face and stuck a finger in his nostril.

"Guys," the teacher called, "stop being silly. This is serious."

But then, the games really began. Over the course of the class, Henry and Stanley got crazier, trying to top each other with each stunt. Henry sat a beaker on his head. Stanley stuck paper in his ears. Toward the end of the class, they each started a fire in the sink and were throwing beakers full of water in the air and catching them. And, at the same moment, they both lost control completely, and the beakers came crashing down on the floor.

"Oops," Stanley said.

"Damn, you guys. You're a disaster!" The teacher ran over to the sinks and turned on the water to put both of the fires out. "Get out of here! Down to the principal's office!"

As Henry and Stanley exited the room, the teacher wrote something down on a clipboard. "Kreiser, you owe fifteen dollars now. And Cassingham, you owe me twelve."

When Henry left school that day Stanley was out by the road again with the same two football players. Henry approached them. The stocky one threw a playful punch at Henry and Henry took the challenge. He danced around in boxing stance. They sparred a bit, taking turns punching and blocking. When done Henry extended his hand. "I'm Henry."

"Miller," the stocky guy said. "And this is Smitty" he pointed to the tall guy.

They started walking along.

"Your crazy Kreiser," Smitty said. "That's why we like you. You don't even care if it's the I.C. Posse. You just go and scratch their car up."

"Yeah," Stanley said. "That's why he's gotta get in the weight room. Got some fights comin' his way."

Henry stopped walking. "Huh?"

"I said you got some fights comin' your way," Stanley repeated.

"Why you say that?"

"Because you keyed that car."

They continued walking along the road toward the parking lot and, one by one, they broke off to their cars. Henry had to walk alone past the Mustang with the stripe and scratch. Rick sat inside. He got out when he saw Henry, so Henry glanced at him and nodded. Rick stared a deadly stare as he watched Henry walk to the Subaru.

Henry was in the kitchen, shirtless, running the blender one evening when Kate walked in. Nearby on the counter was the big plastic jar of Muscle Milk. A stack of muscle magazines were next to it.

"What's all this?" She picked up the Muscle Milk.

"Muscle Milk is protein that repairs the muscles." He poured himself a glass of the white, frothy shake then drank every ounce of it. He smiled with a milk moustache and held his shoulders up in shrug position. "You see my trapezius?"

"Huh?"

"The shoulder muscles that connect to the neck. When you shrug, these are the muscles you use. I worked them out today, and now I'm restoring the protein."

She looked at the price tag on the Muscle Milk. "*Thirty dollars?* And the magazines... how much were they?"

"You know, a few bucks apiece. But I'm learning."

"Learning how to make big muscles? Don't you want to save your money for college?"

Henry shrugged.

Kate sat. "How you doing so far in school, Henry?"

"Great. I told you I was gonna be the best kid."

"Good. I'm looking forward to seeing your report card."

Henry turned on the blender. "*Huh?*" He pointed at the blender. "I can't hear you!"

"Your report card."

"Oh yeah," he said loudly over the sound of the blender. "This is called Muscle Milk!" He held his shoulders up in a shrug. "And these are my trapezius muscles!"

She threw up her hands and walked away. "This kid!"

On a Saturday night Henry drove down the Levittown Parkway with Stanley in the passenger seat and Miller and Smitty in the bed of the Subaru. Henry took a long drink of a 16-ounce Budweiser can and passed it. They pulled into the Fairless Hills Shopping Center and cruised around the parking lot for a bit, watching the other cars. They got out and hung out in front of the Fashion Bug.

At Neon Nights, the club kids crowded in. Stanley, Miller and Smitty stood against a wall and watched the action on the dance floor. Henry took to the floor right away and danced in front of some girls. Then he saw the

Latin girls and with them, the Fotomat girl. When a Hammer song started, a crowd surged onto the floor. A black kid started the Running Man and others backed away. Henry jumped into the circle and started his wild moves. He approached the black kid, face to face. He pumped his fist. Henry was a bit stiff with his new muscles but still had it. He jumped on the horse, smacked its rear and rode away. The black kid stumbled. Henry threw in two pelvis thrusts and slapped the butt. The crowd cheered.

Stanley and the others nearly fell on the floor laughing. They ran onto the dance floor as the song finished and danced in the crowd to the new song. Henry danced with them for a moment then sought out the Fotomat girl. He swaggered and pushed his coif back when he saw her. He danced directly in front of her, and her friends backed away. He moved closer to her, held his arms in the air, swaying into her comfort zone and back out again. He swayed in again.

She smiled. "You got rid of your glasses," she said.

"Huh?"

"Your glasses."

"I don't wear glasses anymore."

"I see that."

"Contact lenses. You know, in your ..." He pointed at his eyes.

"I know," she laughed. "I know what contacts are."

When the song finished, she walked back to her friends.

Henry approached Stanley and the others. A couple high-hair girls in miniskirts were there. Stanley stood back. "You on that chick?" he asked Henry.

A slow song came on. As Henry rushed to the Fotomat girl, the Chris DeBurgh song started—"Lady in Red." Henry was smooth and calm but the moment he took her hand in hers, his swagger disappeared and his palms sweat. The song was about a man in love—a heart devoted to the person in his arms. It was complete and utter love. Henry and the girl danced face to face. When they touched chest to chest Henry surged. A dizzy sensation struck him. "What nationality are you?" he asked, breathing a little heavy.

"Puerto Rican and Italian. You?"
"German and Irish."
"Yeah?"
"Yeah. How old are you?" he asked her.
"Eighteen. How old are you?"
"Uh ..." He paused for a long moment. "Umm ... shmarmteen. I'm Henry. What's your name?"
"I'm Esther. How old did you say you were?"
"Umm ... shmarmteen."
"You're mumbling. I'm sorry. I didn't hear you."
"Umm ... eighteen," Henry said, clearly.

After the club closed, Henry and Esther sat on a curb in the parking lot. Cars on Levittown Parkway whizzed by behind them. Stanley and the others sat in the window of V&S Pizza and looked over toward them occasionally. Henry was struck silent and only asked an occasional question to keep her talking.

"I was born in Puerto Rico but moved to Trenton when I was three—with my mom."

"Your dad?"

"He stayed in Puerto Rico."

A long silence followed. She wasn't looking at him so he examined her from head to toe. Her black curls lay on one shoulder, exposing her neck. Her lips were full and calm. She fiddled gently with a buckle on her shoe. "My mom works at Woolworth's at the mall."

She turned and touched his hand, looking up at him, then cupped his coif with her open hand. "I like your haircut. Did you get a perm?"

"No... my hair is naturally curly."

She looked in his eyes, craning her neck. He kissed her on the cheek and backed away.

He heard banging and looked over at the window of V&S Pizza. Stanley, Miller and Smitty were there, waving and laughing. They pointed at Esther and made kissy faces.

Henry stood up. "Want to walk over to the lake?"

They walked together, across the road, to Lake Caroline.

"Watch for the goose poop," he said. They sat on a picnic table.

"How about you?" she asked. "Where do you live?"

"Near here. With my sister."

"Your sister?" she asked. "Where are your mom and dad?"

"They died when I was young. I moved around a lot. I went to a boarding school for kids from broken families."

"Sorry." She touched his hand.

"And now I'm here in Levittown. I go to Truman High School."

She pulled her hand away. "Wait...you're still in high school? I thought you were eighteen."

"I am, but I... I had to... I mean, I was a little behind because I moved around a lot."

"Oh. Well I thought you were finished."

"It's my last year but I have a job at a factory. We make bingo chips. I make good money. So—"

"Bingo chips?" She giggled.

"What's so funny?" he asked defensively.

"Nothing." She smiled warmly.

"Where did *you* go to high school?" Henry asked.

"I went to Trenton Central High... but I dropped out."

"Will you go back?" He took her hand now.

"I'll get my GED, I guess."

The lake was like glass. Back porch lights from the homes on the other side reflected on the surface.

"You don't think less of me, do you?" she asked. "...for not finishing high school?"

Henry turned to her with an earnest look in his eyes. "No— of course not. You don't think less of me for still being in high school, do you?"

"No. You'll finish, I'm sure. I am glad you're eighteen, though."

He leaned in, kissed her on the lips—then moved his body closer and kissed with parted lips. He felt her soft and open so closed his eyes and let his mind wander—he saw a beach and water. He opened his eyes again and saw her closed eyes. He spun around her in his mind, wrapped his arms around her side and pulled her in close. After several moments he released her and they looked into each other's eyes.

"Gotta go," she said. "My friend is waiting for me."

"She doesn't like me, does she?" Henry said, blinking away the emotion from the kiss.

"She's just tough, you know. She doesn't understand what I see in white boys."

"White boys?"

"Yeah, you're a white boy. I'm not exactly white."

"Oh. I know," he said.

"That's all I meant."

He thought about it. "You think I'm..."

"I gotta go," she interrupted.

"Wait!" His voice squeaked with excitement so he coughed to correct it and distract her from it. "Can I have your number?"

She rifled through her purse and found a pen and paper. She scribbled a number down and handed it to him.

"So, I guess I could call you tomorrow at 3:30," he said.

She laughed, leaned in and kissed him on the cheek then darted off. He watched her cross the road back over to the shopping center, worrying for a moment that she would get hit by a car. Then he sat on the picnic bench and watched the water. Ripples from a fish scattered the reflecting lights. After a moment of pensive silence he went back across the road and entered V&S Pizza.

He grabbed a slice and sat with the guys. They were boisterous and rowdy. Henry was quiet and looked out the window at the passing cars as he ate his pizza. Miller and Smitty left eventually, leaving Stanley and Henry.

"Dude," Stanley said. "Why you so quiet all of a sudden?"

Henry shrugged. "Nothing."

As they headed to Henry's car, Stanley stopped dead in

his tracks. "Get ready," he said. "Two on three!"

"Huh?" Henry saw Rick and his two I.C. Posse buddies approaching quickly across the parking lot.

When they were close, Stanley ran at them, throwing punches. It started sloppy and only an occasional fist actually connected at first. One of them fell. Then Stanley fell. Henry froze—he couldn't believe his eyes. Stanley got up and looked at Henry. "Come on, man!" he said. "What the fuck are you doing?"

Henry flinched; he almost moved, but his feet stayed planted in place. He looked at his feet and then looked at Stanley, who was now getting attacked by all three. But Stanley slapped and punched aggressively and quickly knocked Rick back onto his butt, where he sat too dazed to get back up. Stanley continued hitting the other two randomly as they attacked him. "Kreiser! You gonna help me?"

Henry's face was filled with fear.

Stanley knocked a second one down before turning to take on the last one. He swept at his ankles and tripped the guy. As the last guy was falling toward the ground, Stanley brought an elbow to his head, finishing him off.

"Let's go!" Stanley said.

They ran to Henry's car.

As he drove off, he saw blood on Stanley's hands. When they pulled onto the Levittown Parkway, a bottle came smashing down on the road in front of Henry's car. He skidded to a stop. Another bottle smashed into the truck bed of the Brat.

"Go!" Stanley yelled.

Henry hit the gas with a screech.

"Dude!" Stanley said. "You can't just stand there – it was two on three... I needed your help!"

Henry shrugged while keeping his eyes on the road.. "I was about to get in there. I mean I almost jumped in, but... then you suddenly beat them all." He laughed. "Man, you kicked their asses!"

"Well, next time jump in. Seriously— if you're gonna key his car, you better be ready to fight."

"Oh. I will. I mean ... I completely was ready. And I would have helped if you'd needed it."

Stanley stared at him. "Dude. You fucking pissed your pants."

Henry fumbled with the rearview mirror. He looked at his own eyes in the mirror. "I know, man. I'm sorry. I did."

"Why?"

"I don't know. I haven't been in that many fights."

"This would have been a good place to start. Next time, you gotta do it." He punched Henry on the shoulder lightly. "You'll see—it's fun. You gotta work on the agility thing, and you'll see it'll come naturally."

Stanley talked about who he hit and when.

Henry looked ahead. He popped in a tape. A Hammer melody started with a rap dance rhythm. Then rapping started.

"Off with the Hammer," Stanley demanded. "Where's my Public Enemy tape?"

"In the glove box."

Stanley pulled out the Hammer tape and put in Public Enemy. On the stereo a man called out "Brothas and sistas" once, then again. And the music started with a hard beat and electronic whistling. It was an overtly aggressive sound as a rapid beat with snares traded jabs with a record scratching. The song, which was absent of melody, struck Henry in a new way. The aggressive rhythm touched a place untouched. It wasn't a rhythm that provoked in him a desire to dance; rather it was a rhythm that sparked the need to fight. Henry looked at Stanley's bloody hands and then watched the road ahead. He let the music nod his head. *Pissed my fucking pants*, he thought. *I'm a fucking sissy. I don't even know. I know. I don't. I should have fucking ... I know how to fuck the fuck up. Fuck. Fuck!*

At home, after Henry finished doing push-ups, he put the Public Enemy tape in the stereo. He peeled off his sweaty shirt and flexed in the mirror. He held his fists in front of his face. then punched at the mirror and dodged. *Body blow*, he thought. *Jab. Jab. Body blow. Right hook. Agility is the key.* He dodged some more. He stepped forward quickly and stepped back and to the side. He threw a rapid series of punches, dodged, and then stood high to watch his enemy fall. He kicked him while he was down. *That's how you fucking do it*, he thought.

As he gathered himself, and the euphoria of winning the imaginary fight empowered him, he spotted his coif out of the corner of his eye in the mirror. He turned and looked at himself. His hair now glistened with sweat, and the curls from the perm loosened up a bit. He moved closer to look and reached to touch it but stopped short and just stared at it. *My fucking hair is awesome*, he thought.

He grabbed the Public Enemy cassette tape and examined the pictures on the leaflet inside. They all wore hats, mostly baseball caps, and were dressed in a uniquely militant hip-hop style. He set the leaflet down on the desk and grabbed the MC Hammer cassette. He pulled out the leaflet and set it down next to the Public Enemy one. Hammer's style, on the whole, was flamboyant—high hair and ridiculously baggy pants. Henry looked back and forth from one to the other.

At dinner the next evening Henry put down his fork suddenly. "Thank you, Kate," he said suddenly.

"For what?" She glanced at Jack.

"For taking me out of Milton Hershey and trusting me."

"You're welcome. I knew I could."

"I'm very happy right now, with my job and with my friends at school."

"Good. I'm looking forward to seeing the report card."

Henry got up and put his dish in the sink. Jack watched him.

"She's looking forward to seeing the report card, Henry," Jack said.

Henry nodded. "Yeah!" He went to his bedroom.

At school, Stanley pulled Henry aside in the hall. "Listen – it's gonna happen tonight!"

"What're you talkin' about?"

"The fight. We're gonna bang. Rick threw a fucking

rock through my window. My dad was reading the newspaper and a fucking rock landed at his feet."

"What?!"

"Yeah! So, they're having a party tonight, and we're gonna clear it out."

"We?"

Stanley paused. "What – you're not down?"

"Yeah. I'm down, but... I mean, I gotta go. I just gotta do some—"

"You're already pissin' in your pants. Listen to you!"

"No, I'm not," Henry said, defensively. "I'm just sayin'"

"I'll come pick you up around nine, so be ready. We'll go in my brother's car because they'll recognize your car. They're fucking finished!"

"Ah, man. Let's—"

"See you tonight, Kreiser." Stanley grabbed Henry's arm. "Right?"

"Yeah. Of course." Henry sighed as Stanley walked away.

That evening Stanley drove slowly through the Pinewood section of Levittown. Henry guzzled some beer then passed the can to Smitty. Miller downed one, crushed the can on his forehead, and burped a sentence: "We goin' fuck them up."

Henry looked in the rearview mirror and saw two other cars following at the same pace and making the same turns.

They soon stopped and parked all three cars a few houses down from the party. They sat in the car, drank more beer, and listened to rap for a few minutes. They could hear rock and roll and dozens of loud voices spilling out into the street from the party.

Stanley punched the steering wheel and got out of the car suddenly. All three cars emptied onto the street. There were ten of them in total and most were big, athletic types—the whole football team. Henry ran to catch up and walk beside Stanley as they all flooded into the house quickly and without knocking. Stanley, still in the lead, saw Rick and other I.C. Posse members in the kitchen—all with the sleeve up-sleeve down dress code in place. A few menacing looking hairy men in their twenties were among Rick and the high school kids. Before Rick became aware of their presence Stanley grabbed him by the back of the shirt. He yanked the shirt over Rick's head and started pounding his head with his fists. Smitty and Miller started fighting others—easily identifying the I.C. Posse members and randomly punching them in face. The girls in the house were terrified and screaming. Two of them threw beer cans at their unwelcome guests.

Henry pushed a smaller guy into the bathroom and shut the door. When he turned around, only a few girls were left in the kitchen, and they glared at him. "Sorry about this," he said. One of the girls threw a full can of beer at him, but he dodged it and it slammed against the bathroom door. He ran out front of the house.

In the front yard, Henry could see that the football players were, on the whole, beating the I.C. Posse. But he was startled to see Stanley in the mess now losing to Rick. As Henry approached to help, he did a dance. He stepped forward with clenched fists. He stepped back. He waved his hands wildly, hoping that Rick would let go of Stanley. Stanley's eyes began to glaze and he was moving in slow motion. Rick paused and looked over at Henry—right in the eyes. "What are you gonna do, spaz?" he said. "Hit yourself in the head?"

Henry's eyes flashed red. A fierce unfamiliar anger ripped into him. He moved forward without an ounce of hesitation. He charged, cocking his fist far behind his back, then swung it around and slammed it into the side of Rick's head. Rick's arms went limp immediately, his shoulders dropped, and he fell to the ground. And Henry's fury continued. He took a running jump and brought his foot down on Rick's head then looked down at him. "That's right, I'm a spaz, motherfucker!" Henry hacked and spit at Rick, but it mostly fell on his own chin. Then he froze in disbelief when he saw Rick was nearly unconscious and had blood coating his hair and trickling down his neck. He was trying to say something but his words were slurring and lips and tongue just flapped around making grunting noises.

Henry grabbed Stanley and helped him up. Back on his feet again, Stanley lunged forward as if he was going to kick Rick in the head but then stopped when he saw him struggling to lift his head off the ground.

Stanley turned to Henry. "What the *fuck* was that?"

"I don't know. I mean ..." Henry said.

"It was fucking awesome! Let's get out of here!"

In the car, they cleaned the blood off of themselves. Henry sat in the back seat and stared off into space. Stanley drove off. "Did you guys see Kreiser? He did some kind of fucking running punch and knocked Rick the fuck out... in *one shot*!"

"Ehhh...," Henry said hesitantly, looking out the window.

"No, Kreiser, you fucked him up and saved my ass!"

"Whatever." Henry's voice had little enthusiasm compared to Stanley's.

"Don't gimme that, Kreiser!" Stanley looked at Henry in the rearview mirror. "Why are you downplaying it? Be proud that you finally kicked his ass!"

Henry sighed. "I don't even know why we did that."

"Whatever, Kreiser. Don't feel bad—you're the one who started it anyway when you keyed his car. You reap what you sow, man."

Henry called Esther one evening that week, and they talked for twenty minutes. "Want to go out sometime?" he asked her. She hesitated. "Come on," he persisted, "I'll come over there to Trenton."

That weekend Henry drove across the Route 1 bridge to Trenton, New Jersey. Following written instructions, he pulled off the highway into a neighborhood of row homes—some small and modestly maintained and others small and falling. Latin music with big bass pumped from little Toyotas with tinted windows. With each one he passed, the bass shook Henry's car windows. He pulled down Bayard Street, lined with quiet brick and vinyl-sided two-story homes, and struggled to parallel park the

Subaru. A teenage boy with gelled black hair, and gold chains laying over top of a turtleneck, sat on a stoop—watching Henry back up and pull forward a dozen times. He laughed when Henry was finally in place—the Subaru protruding out into the street.

Henry approached a brick home and rang. He was startled when Esther opened the door. Her black dress, ruffled down to her knees, showed her curves. Her calves exposed olive skin and hair was wet and black, like oil. Henry extended his hand nervously but she looked at it, giggled then leaned forward and gave him a hug. In the living room, a black kid was watching TV. "That's my foster brother," Esther said. "Willy, meet Henry."

Willy, who wore a bandanna and a gold chain, looked up and nodded.

Henry stood speechless for a moment. He saw a tattoo of a spider on Willy's neck. "I'm ... I'm Henry. Nice to meet you." Henry stared at him, as if he expected the conversation to continue.

Willy shot him a look. "Need something from me?" he asked.

"I... was... just... nothing." Henry went with Esther into her bedroom. He sat on the bed while she excused herself for a minute. He looked out the window, which was covered in clear plastic, at a brick wall. Esther returned with two glasses of iced tea, and put some music on. The song had a fast dance beat and passionate lyrics—a style Henry hadn't heard before.

"Who's that kid out there?" he asked.

"I told you, he's my foster brother. My mom took him in a few months ago but she is never here so I'm stuck feeding him and keeping an eye on him."

Henry nodded. The chorus of the song began. The fast rhythm and vocals excited Henry. "Who is this?"

"Oh, this? It's T.L.R. You haven't heard of freestyle music?"

"No, I did. Yeah, I've heard of it." He stood and danced a little bit. "They're great." The beat was not what he was used to dancing to, so he tripped a little.

"Like this," she said. "Don't bounce." Her movements were more fluid than his and she froze for a millisecond on each beat before continuing.

He tried to move with her but continued to bounce.

"Don't bounce," she said.

Then, he moved his hips in a kind of sexy way, mimicking her movements. While he was dancing his gaze lowered to her waist—which moved back and forth and up and down. He bit his lip, trying to focus on dancing but her waist was having a hypnotic effect on him and was provoking pangs of lust. He started to reach for her.

"Guys aren't supposed to move like that," she said.

He stopped dancing and pulled the needle off the record. "Just let me dance."

"Well, you can't do it like that," she laughed.

"What's funny?"

"You're funny, Henry." She gently touched his nose with her finger. "Let's go for a walk."

As they walked past the living room, Henry looked in at Willy. They stepped outside and walked down the street to Columbus Park. "That's where I buy my Wigwams," Esther told him, pointing to a store on the corner with colorful sweaters in the window. They crossed and went into the park.

"What are Wigwams?" Henry asked.

She laughed. "Socks! You know... thick ones that you wear outside of pants? You have a lot to learn."

They sat down on a bench.

"No– I mean I forgot that they were called Wigwams."

"It's okay; you're still in high school."

"So? That doesn't matter."

She giggled. He moved in on her quickly, kissing her lips. He spun around her. His novice lips danced a bit too much so she bit his lip gently. He slowed down. She nibbled him more and played with him. Her dancing tongue made him spin.

He took a deep breath, looking in her eyes. "I love you," he said. He leaned in to kiss again.

She stopped and pulled back. "What?"

"I love you."

"Oh," she said with surprise. "Really?" She looked over at the Wigwam store. "Who are you?" she asked, inching away.

"Who am I?" he glanced at her waist to try to understand if she was just shifting in place or moving away from him.

"Yeah – who *are* you, Henry Kreiser? Why are you so serious about starting something with a Trenton girl. You're a good-looking guy... aren't there girls in Pennsylvania?"

He shrugged, annoyed at the change of tone in her voice. "Don't ask that. I don't know."

"You don't know?"

"Well," he shifted toward her closing the gap and pressing his chest against her shoulder. "I know you're beautiful. What else do I need to know?"

"Aw." She kissed him.

A few weeks later Stanley drove with Henry, Smitty and Miller down the Mill Creek Parkway, sharing a couple beers.

"Hold them down," Stanley said. They passed the Bristol Township Police Station and turned onto Green Avenue where they found the party—in a two-car detached garage. Music and chatter spilled out into the street. Inside there were a half dozen guys in hooded sweatshirts gathered around a kerosene heater. Henry recognized most of them from school but didn't know any of them by name. Rap music was on too loud for the little speakers.

"The bitches will be here soon, boys!" the host held a beer high in the air. "Beer is in the back!"

As the party went on, the music got louder. Stanley and Miller were hitting on the only two girls and their progress seemed promising from what Henry could see. One of the girls had her hand on Stanley's arm. Henry's beer buzz turned into a bit of a trance with the loud music. He was soon talking with a guy in a flannel shirt as others circled around the kerosene heater. The music changed to rock. Guns N' Roses sang "Sweet Child O' Mine." Henry suddenly felt unsettled. The little speakers crackling from the stress of high volume magnified the feeling. He noticed that the guys in hooded sweatshirts were all gone, and others in flannels now gathered around the heater. He saw the sleeve-up sleeve-down I.C. Posse dress code on several of them and was startled. Then, when Henry saw Rick enter he immediately scanned the room for any sign Stanley, Miller or Smitty. He figured Stanley and Miller were off with the girls somewhere but couldn't account for Smitty. The volume of the music was turned up even higher now and Henry couldn't hear anything else. The chorus of "Sweet Child O' Mine" raged.

Henry went straight for the door to leave. But Rick stepped in his way. He got in Henry's face and started yelling something that was incomprehensible to Henry with the music so loud.

"What are you talking about?" Henry asked as loudly as he could.

Without answering Rick cocked his fist back and swung at Henry. Henry saw it coming but had nowhere to move so he dropped toward the floor. As he went down Rick's fist landed on the side of his head. Henry popped back up and returned a punch, leaping over toward the heater where Rick had moved. He missed Rick's head and hit his shoulder. As he stumbled forward Henry sensed the circle of I.C. Posse guys closing in on him so he sought an escape. Before he could find one, though, punches began flying in from every direction, striking him in the back and in the side of the head. He fell to the floor, dazed. When he tried to break his fall his hands landed on the scolding hot metal of the kerosene heater, so he pulled them back and fell further—his face now slamming into the hot metal. He smelled kerosene. He pushed the heater away and lifted himself up, escaping from the dog pile.

Fear, fury, and confusion gripped Henry as he scrambled across the garage floor, getting back up on his feet. He touched his mouth and felt blood flowing. He found the garage doors and yanked to open one but it was locked. He jumped to the other one and found it too was locked. As he searched for a way to unlock the door he glanced back and saw that his attackers were now converging on him. He searched more in a panic, found the lock and knocked it with his knuckle, successfully unlocking it. It was too late, though, as he had to turn and defend himself. As Rick threw another punch somebody else tackled him from the side. It was Smitty. And the garage door that Henry had unlocked suddenly opened. Stanley and Miller stormed inside, throwing punches at anybody in front of Henry. They took out a few I.C. Posse members, but they were outnumbered significantly. Henry, dazed and drunk, had blood all over his face and on his chest.

Miller grabbed him and they retreated together out into the street. As their opponents followed, the fight broke off into several small ones separated by parked cars. Henry saw a handful of guys in hooded sweatshirts had returned and were fighting the I.C. Posse members too. A car window shattered under a flying elbow and the car alarm went off causing everyone to stop for a moment. Before the fight resumed, sirens sounded out. "Police!" somebody yelled. The fight was over in a few short seconds as most of the kids disappeared into the dark of the surrounding yards.

Stanley pulled up in his car and Miller helped Henry in. "Fuck!" Stanley said, as they drove away. "They fucked you up, Kreiser. Your fucking face is fucked the fuck up! We'll fuck up those motherfuckers!"

"It's not that bad. They didn't—I fell. I mean, my face hit that kerosene heater. They wanted to fuck me up. They dog-piled me."

"Whatever, man. Stop that. They fucked you up, and we're gonna fuck them up!"

Henry pulled down the sun visor. He flicked on the inside light and looked in the vanity mirror. "What the fuck?!" he said. There was a huge gash across his lip, and smears of blood covered his chin and neck. The wound was already black and sticky.

They dropped him off at home. "Don't worry, Kreiser. We're gonna get 'em back really hard this time. You just say the word, and we're with you."

Henry entered the house and went to the bathroom. In the bright light, he saw the gash on his lip in full view for the first time. He touched it and winced in pain. He went to the kitchen and pulled out a liter of rum from the top of the cabinet. He put some on the gash, drank a little, and looked closer. Anger logic took over—judge and jury of the mind. For several minutes he examined his lip and the facts. He pulled off his shirt. He drank more and got drunker quickly. He scrunched his face in anger. "My fucking face is fucked!" He grabbed his keys and ran out of the house, shirtless and shoeless. When he got to the car, he reached under the seat to see if the knife was still there. He felt the sharp point then pulled the knife up and put in on the passenger seat. "I'll fuck them up," he said. "I'll fuck them the fuck up."

Henry drove maniacally on a rum-fueled mission. When he stopped at a light, he flipped the mirror down and drank more rum. The lip had become a monstrosity of scabs. His face around the wound was swollen and discolored. He drove fast and drank more as he passed the police station. Back on Green Avenue, all was quiet. The garage doors were closed but a light was on inside. Henry pulled his car to look to the side door of the garage. A lone man—an older guy—turned off the light inside and walked back to the house. Henry put down the passenger window.

"Hey, who's party was this?" Henry asked.

"There's no party anymore, son. It's already over—you missed it."

"No, I said who's *was* it?"

"Just some kids. Go on home now. It's all over."

"I'm not going anywhere." Henry put the car in neutral and yanked up the emergency brake. He got out. "Well, you tell whoever started the fight in there that he's gonna pay for it! Some pond person named Rick that drives a Mustang."

The door of the house shot open and two kids came

out. It was Rick and one of his buddies. They came running across the lawn to the car. Henry reached in and grabbed the knife. He whipped it out and held it like a sword.

"Yo, dude," Rick said, noticing Henry's bare chest and bare feet. He saw a wild look in Henry's eyes. "Put the knife away!"

Henry just stared at him, and then looked at the older man.

"Hey kid!" the old man pointed at Henry. "What are you doing with that?"

Henry froze as they stared at him. Then he got slowly back in the car. He put the knife on the seat. "On my way," he said to them. "Sorry!"

He drove slowly off Green Avenue and turned onto the police station road. He put both hands on the wheel and drove easily. Halfway home, he pulled onto the gravel on the side of the Mill Creek Parkway. He vomited out the window down the side of the car. As he finished vomiting he began to feel the cold November night on his bare feet and back. He shivered uncontrollably the rest of the ride home. Back at home, he took the knife inside, put it on his dresser and looked at it for a long moment. Then he went to the kitchen and put it away.

In chemistry class, Stanley started his regular antics. He put a beaker inside of a beaker inside of a beaker and then poured in a blue liquid. He pretended to drink it, staring at Henry with crossed eyes. But Henry didn't respond.

"What's your problem, Kreiser?" Stanley asked after class.

"You mess around too much. That's what."

"*I* mess around too much? You're the goofball, not me."

"Whatever," Henry said dismissively.

Stanley threw an arm over his shoulder. "Come on, bonehead. Let's go lift. You're looking kind of skinny."

Henry pushed Stanley's hand off his shoulder. "Stop, dude. I really can't. I got other things I gotta do."

"You see? You're gonna give up on lifting just as you begin to get some muscles?"

"Fuck you, Stanley. You see my fucking lip? Right? You see it? I got jumped by a bunch of dudes. And what did my fucking trapezius muscles do to help me? And what did your pecs do to help me?"

"I'm sorry, man. I wasn't paying attention."

"And, so I got my ass beaten."

"You were just outnumbered. If any of them were one on one, you would have—"

"Whatever. The point is, muscles are useless in this case. Why go through all that trouble of lifting weights if something like this can happen?"

"So what are you gonna do? Carry a knife? A gun?"

"What if they smashed my head in and I got killed? That happens sometimes, you know."

"You're gonna get a gun, aren't you," Stanley said.

"Nah, man. I'm just gonna stay away from it all."

On Thanksgiving Day a week later Henry ran to pick up eggnog at Kate's request then returned home to find Byron standing in the living room, home from college for the long weekend.

"Holy crap," Byron said to Henry. "What happened to your face?"

"I fell when I was dancing at a party."

"You mean you fell on somebody's fist." Byron threw a fake punch at him.

"No! My face hit a kerosene heater."

Henry went to the kitchen to put the eggnog in the refrigerator and Byron followed. Kate and Jack were scooping stuffing from a turkey.

"Nothing but trouble," Kate said. "D's and F's on his first report card! I'm regretting taking him out of Hershey."

The rest of the family soon arrived. After dinner they ate pumpkin pie and drank coffee, finishing up long overdue conversations.

"So when the mortgage broker told us how much we'd actually be paying," Chuck explained to Kate, "we just saved up for another year. It made it all worthwhile."

A long silence followed. To that point, Henry was quiet.

"You gotta straighten the fuck up," Byron said to him, breaking the silence. "Or you're going back to Hershey."

"Huh?" Henry looked around. The others were all watching.

Henry got up from the table, grabbed his jacket, and walked out. Byron followed him. They walked down to the park at the end of their street, where there was an elementary school.

"Dude, what's your problem?" Byron asked.

"I don't have a problem." Henry sat on a bleacher next to the ball field.

"This reminds me exactly of the Milt... we've been at this exact point before!"

"At what point?" Henry asked defensively. "Everything is fine."

"The point where you are fucking up, and I'm telling you to straighten up. But it keeps getting worse, rather than better."

"Well, then maybe you should just give up."

"No. I want to know what happened." Byron pointed at his face.

"I told you; I fell."

"I know you didn't fall. You got busted in the lip because you were trying to be tough."

Henry shrugged.

"So, what's next?" Byron wanted to know.

"I don't know." Henry shrugged.

"Well, whatever you decide to do next, I'm here to tell you to do the right thing."

"What is that supposed to mean?"

"I mean you obviously have not been happy with yourself." Byron poked him in the chest gently.

"You're crazy. I'm happy with myself."

"Well, then, what's your problem? Why do you try so hard to be some punk kid?"

Henry shrugged. "I don't know."

"You *do* know," Byron insisted.

"I don't know, dude. It's like I try to be cool, but people keep fucking with me."

"Are they fucking with you, or are you fucking with them?"

Henry shrugged. The rest of the family arrived and sat down on the bleachers with Henry and Byron.

"You have five brothers and sisters, Henry," Chuck said. "You know that?"

"I know."

"Well, use us. You're driving Kate and Byron crazy. So if you need something, use me."

"Or me," Liz said.

"Me, too," said Teddy.

"I will," Henry said, with less sincerity than the offers he was responding to.

CHAPTER 9

Henry left twelve messages on Esther's answering machine throughout the week. She never called back. The following Saturday he went to Oxford Valley Mall and found Woolworth's. He wandered around, looking at the clerks—reading their nametags. In the sporting goods section, he found a Latin woman around fifty years old. He took a close look at her while she was restacking boxed basketballs on a shelf. On her nametag was written "Sanchez."

"Do you have a daughter named Esther?" Henry asked her.

She froze. "Yes. What happened?"

"Oh, nothing. I'm Henry. I was at your house last week and she told me you work here."

"Oh, Henry. Yeah, she told me about you."

"I just thought I would stop by and meet you since me and Esther are ... you know ..."

"You are what?"

"I mean, we are ... we're going out. I mean, we went out together."

She laughed and began stacking basketballs again. "What happened to your lip."

"Just ... nothing. Fell and hit a kerosene heater."

"Esther's coming in an hour to take me to lunch. Why don't you wait for her?"

Henry wandered. He looked at bed sheets and then perused mops and bottles of bleach. After a bit, he went back the sporting goods section. When Esther arrived,

Henry was looking at a badminton set. He looked up and saw a confused look on her face.

"Henry?"

"I was just shopping and I—"

"My mom works here."

"I know. You told me. I was shopping in the mall, so I decided to stop by and say hi to her. And then she told me you were coming."

"What happened to your lip?"

"Nothing. Fell and hit a kerosene heater."

She took a closer look and touched his cheek. "Whoa, it's pretty bad."

"It's not so bad," he said, dismissively.

"I got your messages. All of them."

"Oh." He set down the badminton set and took her hand. "Why didn't you call back?"

"It was Black Friday. So everybody was dropping off their Thanksgiving pictures, and it took me long to close."

"Let's go to Cape May this weekend," he squeezed her hand.

"You're crazy. It's too cold for the shore."

"Come on. I wanna show you where my family used to go. Plus, it'll be all decorated for Christmas."

"I don't know. Sunday's my only day off, and I need to do laundry."

"Esther! Laundry? Come on! We'll play Skee-Ball."

Her mom came down the aisle. "There you are."

"Hi, Mom. Did you meet Henry?"

"I did. Such a nice, *young* man."

"Can you do my laundry on Sunday? He wants to take me to Cape May."

"Cape May? It's too cold for the shore."

Henry laughed.

Esther laughed too. "That's what I said, but he says some stuff is open."

"Sure. I can do your laundry if you want to go."

On Sunday they drove from Trenton through the Pine Barrens and then turned onto the Garden State Parkway. Gray sky hung over marsh grasses and empty inlets.

Esther put her hand over Henry's. "There's nobody on the road."

"That's why it's so nice."

"It's a little creepy," she said.

The state highway turned into a Cape May county byway. In Cape May, they drove around a bit, slowing down to look at Victorian homes all decorated. Fresh Christmas wreaths hung on front doors. Handmade Santas sat next to straw-littered, life-sized mangers. On the boardwalk they went to the only place open and played Skee-Ball under a ceiling of stuffed animals. Henry acted goofy, rolling the ball behind his back and under his leg. Then Esther started winning, so he suddenly got serious. And his balls began going in all the right holes.

"You're supposed to let the girl win, dummy," she said as he gathered his tickets from the attendant. He started perusing a cabinet full of plastic guns. "I know," he said. "I mean, I wanted to win you something. That's why I tried so hard. Pick something."

"No. You go ahead."

He chose two plastic handguns. He stuffed one in his waistband and then handed her the other.

"Why would you choose guns?" she asked. She held it between her fingers like she was afraid it would go off.

Henry shrugged. "What else was I going to choose? A stuffed animal?"

For lunch they went to a pizza place a block back from the beach. After finishing their cheese steaks and French fries, Henry looked in the mirror next to their booth and saw the reflection of another mirror in the booth across from them. He saw his and Esther's reflection go on and on—black curls, blond coif, black curls, blond coif—infinitely.

After lunch they drove a bit farther, to the village of Cape May Point at the end of the peninsula. They stopped in front of a small, one-story home with a sand-and-grass lawn. A sign out front said "Restawhile."

"This is where we used to stay," he said.

"Who?" she asked, leaning over to look out his window.

"My whole family when I was little. It only has two rooms, but there's a little mini-cottage in the back that all of us kids stayed in."

"How many brothers and sisters do you have?"

"Three brothers and two sisters."

"Let me guess: you're the youngest."

"How did you know?"

She shrugged. "It's obvious."

He drove on. "What do you mean, it's obvious?"

"I mean, you can just tell. You're the baby."

"A baby?!"

"I didn't say you *are* a baby. I said you were *the* baby. And that's why you're sensitive, too."

Henry shot her a glance as he turned onto another road lined with cottages. "All right, you really need to stop saying those things or I'm gonna cry."

She laughed.

They pulled around the corner and parked next to the little gray wooden church where his family had told him about his father's impending death almost a decade prior. He stared at the church for a long moment. "I ... this church is where ... this is where ..."

"What?"

"Nothing. Let's go for a walk."

They walked up to the beach but found that much of the sand had been washed away. They climbed over rocks that were piled to fortify the dunes. On the other side of a jetty, the beach was in better shape. When Henry saw the big, concrete World War II bunker up ahead, he jumped down onto the sand and ran.

Esther followed. "Let's go back to the car," she called. "It's cold!" The sound of the crashing waves concealed her plea.

Henry climbed the steps onto the bunker, pulling out his plastic pistol. "Get your gun out!" he yelled down to her. "The Germans are coming!" He ducked down out of sight. "Come on!"

She climbed the steps. Henry was sitting on the ground in the corner. She sat down next to him. "Warm here, out of the wind," she said, as she leaned into him.

He wrapped his arm around her. A seagull squawked. He glanced up and saw it circling above. "We used to come fishing here," Henry said. "We cast our lines right over the edge."

"Did you ever catch a fish?"

"Oh, yeah. All the time. Big ones" He paused. "I mean, not really. My dad did. But something horrible happened one day."

"What?"

"I had a big fish." He indicated the length with his hands. "But I lost it."

"So? You lost a fish."

"Yeah. But my dad said it probably died. Because of the hook."

"Oh. Poor fish."

"I cried and cried."

"Really? Why?"

"I don't know. It just seemed so cruel. The death. Oh, I remember. I thought about the little baby fish who lost their ... I don't know. It was just so sad to me."

"You were saying something about the little baby fish. What do you mean?"

"I don't know. Nothing."

"No, tell me," she nudged his face toward hers. "That seemed like something important."

"Well, I meant, that was just sad for me to think about the baby fish swimming around with their mom or dad dying with a hook in their mouth because some stupid kid didn't know how to reel him in."

"Oh. So you felt guilty?"

"Yeah. I guess I did."

"That's sweet." She kissed him on the cheek.

They listened to the waves crashing below. "It's cold," he said.

"That's what I've been telling you. Let's go!"

They drove over to Sunset Beach, which faced west across the Delaware Bay, just as the sun was setting. Another car was there. They stopped the car next to a produce stand on sand near a patch of scraggly pines. The stand was boarded up with a sign: "Closed for the Season." Only a tub of rotted Jersey tomatoes was left there. They sat, quietly looking out at the hull of the aging concrete ship that sat broken in the shallow water just beyond the small bay breakers. "And this is where we used to come to watch the sunset," he said.

He turned to her. She kissed his busted lip. Their hands rushed and searched. Her breath echoed in his ear as she kissed it. He felt dizzy. "I had fun today," she whispered.

He looked at her. Her eyes were soft and earnest, her lips red from touch. He touched. They kissed again and he held her close. "I love you," he said.

"I love you, too."

She leaned on his shoulder the whole way back to Trenton, staring ahead at the passing cars' taillights.

Back at her house, as he went up the steps ahead of her, she grabbed his ankles playfully. He tripped and she jumped on top of him, kissing him. They heard the floor creak, so they looked up the steps. Willy was there. "Get a hotel," he said as he went into the living room. Esther went to the bedroom while Henry followed Willy into the living room. Willy was sitting there with his feet up on the coffee table. A dirty plate and fork lay next to his legs.

"That your pistol?" Willy asked, pointing to the plastic gun in Henry's waistband.

"Yeah, popped a cap in some Germans." Henry walked with a bit more of a swagger than normal.

Willy looked him up and down. "You know what's wrong with you?"

Henry laughed. "What?"

"Don't laugh."

"What's wrong with me?"

"You got some muscles, and you think you bad. You walk like a fuckin' rooster. But I know you ain't bad. You just got a couple muscles. And you still skinny."

Henry nodded. He laughed uncomfortably this time. "Oh yeah?"

Willy showed a gold tooth. "I said don't laugh. You wanna see my pistol?"

"Yeah. Sure. Show me."

Willy slowly lifted his shirt, revealing a black steel pistol under the waistband of his pants.

Henry froze. "I... you... uhh..." Henry left for the bedroom.

"What's wrong with you?" Esther asked, when Henry came in and closed the door.

"Ask Willy. He seems to know. Guy's a dick."

"Don't worry about him."

"Listen Esther, he's got a fucking gun." He sat on the bed while keeping an eye on the door.

"So do you."

"No. He has a real gun. A handgun."

"What?"

"Yup. He showed it to me."

"I'll tell him to get the hell out of here." She turned to leave the room.

"No. No," Henry said. "Don't worry about it."

"He can't bring a gun in this house."

"No, don't. Don't say anything." He grabbed her hand and pulled her on the bed next to him. He touched her ear and put his fingers in her hair. She touched his chest. She moved her body against his. Her hair fell across his shoulder and in his face. Her movements were slow as slow goes. He felt the coming urge of her and surged. He got dizzy. She dropped her hand on his lap. He leaned over and kissed her aggressively. He could hardly breathe.

She pulled back and touched his lip. It had cracked and blood coated a tooth. She grabbed a tissue and dabbed his tooth.

They lay back on the bed. Clothes were pulled off; they tangled and wrestled. Pants stuck on shoes were lost. Naked flesh touched naked flesh. Rock-hard white boy lay on brown-skinned belly. He moved in place, chest to chest. On her lips, he breathed out, then in. It tickled her. She chewed his good lip. Pressure built and she opened up. Clumsy boy made pelvis move. A warm and foggy womb they spun—sweat on the brow. Sweat in between them pushed aside. After a few minutes, his eyes rolled back and his tongue went dry. First time made him groan real wild. At point of utmost pleasure, a brief loss of sense, then slow unwind. He collapsed.

As sense returned to their eyes, his weight increased. He rolled off. She got up and went to the bathroom.

"That was so good," he said, shielding his eyes from the lights in the ceiling fan.

She returned from the bathroom. "Huh?"

"I said, that was so good."

"Yeah, it was," she said, with little enthusiasm.

"It was?" He sat up in bed. "I mean, it was really, really good."

"Yeah."

"You don't seem as impressed as ... me," Henry said. "Like, I'm tingling all over."

"Me too." She got on the bed with him and kissed his ear. "Me too."

Henry drove home fast that night, without the radio on. He made his own music. First he hummed, and then he sang. When he was almost home, he changed direction and drove some more, wandering the streets of Levittown in the dark night under yellowish streetlights. He sang more—a quiet song of notes high and long.

* * *

Love grew quickly and strong between the young lovers. A short drive across the Delaware River from Levittown to Trenton kept them close.

On his way to Esther's on the afternoon of Christmas Eve, he stopped at a florist on Bridge Street in Morrisville.

"Roses," he told the florist. "A dozen."

"White or red?" the man asked.

"Yeah. That's fine."

"I asked, white or red? Who are they for?"

"My girlfriend."

"So, red roses say 'I love you.' And white roses say 'You're heavenly' and convey reverence and humility."

"Let's do both," Henry said.

When Henry knocked on the door Esther answered and saw the roses in his hands. "Aw! They're beautiful." She wrapped her arms around his neck and kissed him.

"Listen, Esther …"

"What's wrong?"

"Nothing. I want to ask you something."

"You're so serious."

"This is serious. You want to come to my house for dinner tomorrow?"

"Oh. Christmas dinner?" She sat on the step.

"Do you?"

"I don't know."

"Well, I thought it would be nice if you met my family."

"I'd like to," she said. "But can we wait until another day? I mean, not on such an important day?"

"Come on! That's exactly why it would be a good day for you to meet them. I want to show them how nice you are." He stepped down and stood in front of her so he was eye level with her.

"No, Henry. I'm not ready for that."

"What do you mean, you're not ready? I've met your mother."

"It's not the same," she protested.

"Why is it not the same?"

"It's just not."

He sat down next to her. "Why?"

"Because you came here first," she said. "On your own."

"So? That doesn't even make sense."

"I just don't want to go, okay? I'll tell you when I'm ready." She got up and went upstairs.

AMERICAN SPAZ

Henry sat for a second then grabbed the flowers and followed her up the steps. "Your flowers, Esther!"

* * *

When he returned to school in January, Henry buckled down. A halo of love kept him focused. He was nice to Stanley but stopped partying and drinking with him. And he stopped lifting weights altogether. At the bingo chip factory, he went through the motions to get his paycheck and even opened a bank account. Many evenings and most weekends were quiet time that he spent with Esther, behind the plastic-covered windows in her bedroom. Whenever Willy was home, Henry made sure the bedroom door was securely shut and locked.

On a Sunday evening in March, minutes after he left to go home, Henry realized he'd forgotten something and went back to Esther's house. "I forgot my wallet," he said to Willy at the door. "Where's Esther?"

"In her room."

He found her there, sitting on the bed, with her head in her hands. "What's wrong?" Henry asked.

"Why did you lie to me, Henry?"

"I didn't. I mean, what are you talking about?"

She held his driver's license out in her hand.

"You're only seventeen. When we met you said you were eighteen. And you had a birthday, so I thought you were nineteen now—the same age as me."

"Oh shit. I said... I was... I didn't..." He sat on the bed next to her.

"I told my mom. I told everybody 'He's nineteen. I know he looks younger, but he's nineteen.' And they asked, 'Are you sure, Esther?'"

"I'm sorry." He tried to put his arm over her shoulder but she pulled away.

"But why would you lie about your age?"

"I'm so sorry."

"Why did you lie?"

"I don't know. I don't freakin' know." He put his face in his hands for a second then looked her in the eyes. "I just ... I mean, that was the night we met."

"But you had plenty of opportunities to tell me the truth. It's been almost six months! I was having sex with a sixteen-year-old!"

"I didn't want to interfere. It was always goin' so well."

"What grade are you in?"

"Eleventh," Henry said quietly, turning his head down.

"Oh, my God."

"What?"

"I can't. I mean ... I can. You have another whole year of high school. I'm nineteen. I need some space."

"I have a job."

"But you work only a few hours per week."

"I'll quit school. I can start working full time."

"Jesus, Henry. No. No. Sorry. Go. I need some space."

Henry drove home fast and then sat in the car out front. He banged his head on the steering wheel. He punched the dashboard. *Fuck*, he thought. *Fuck, fuck, fuck.*

The following weeks were the longest of Henry's life. He called Esther often but got the answering machine, and he didn't leave a message. On Easter Sunday, she finally picked up but, after a brief hello, she grew quiet.

"Aw," Henry said. "I wish we were in Cape May again. Remember the sunset?"

"It was so beautiful," she said, reengaging in the conversation. "How has work and school been?"

"Good. I'm doing good at both. And I'm saving some money."

"I wish you were older, Henry. We could really have something good."

He made funny voices of little children and made her laugh. "Can I come over?" he asked.

"No, Henry. We shouldn't."

"Why?"

"We just shouldn't."

That week Henry moped around in school. At the end of one day, he saw Stanley out front. "Hey, man."

"Where you been, Kreiser?"

"You know—just goin' to work and stuff."

"How's your girl?" Stanley asked.

"She ... uh ... well, we're not seeing each other. Ya know? She like—"

"What? You broke up?"

"We're just taking some time."

"Gotcha. Sorry, dude. There're other fish in the sea. In fact, there's a party tonight with lots of little fishes. Why don't you come with us?"

"I really don't want to get into any trouble. I mean, with those I.C. Posse assholes."

"Nah, man. They won't be there. Anyway, that's done. Rick and I came to an agreement. And he really doesn't know it was you that keyed his car."

"Where's the party?"

"At this girl Amanda's house. It's all cheerleaders. It'll be fun."

At the party Henry had a couple beers and kept a low profile. It was mostly pom-pom girls and football guys. Then a blonde girl with a puff of hair high in front pulled him in a bedroom, where a bunch of others were sitting Indian-style in a circle. She sat him down. Stanley came in after them and sat on the other side of the circle.

"I heard you broke up with that Trenton girl," the blonde girl whispered in Henry's ear. She put her hand on his leg.

"We ... we're just taking some time off." He heard a gurgle and then a raucous laugh. He sniffed and smelled a skunk-like smell. He heard the gurgle again. He looked over and saw a foot-tall glass bong with water. Stanley had his lips pressed in the top as somebody else lit the little black kernel.

Henry was startled when he felt the girl's hand move farther up his leg. He looked down at her hand. She grabbed the bong with her other hand when it came to her.

Somebody lit it and she sucked and gurgled. He watched the smoke move rapidly up the column to her lips. Her hand flopped and grazed across his lap as her lungs filled with smoke. He felt a surge. She pulled the bong from her lips and leaned back, closing her eyes. Henry saw the red impression of the bong around her lips as she exhaled a puff of smoke. She licked her lips slowly, until they were shiny wet, and let out a throaty sigh. She rubbed her eyes, laughed, and looked at Henry. "Have some." She handed him the bong.

When he took it, she put both hands on his lap and watched him. She kissed his cheek. Another girl reached over with the lighter. Henry looked around and saw everybody looking at him. Stanley was singing and laughing. The girl began rubbing his upper thigh. His eyes bulged. He dropped his face immediately and brought his lips to the bong. He sucked hard and fast and long.

"Dude!" Stanley stopped singing. "Settle down. You're gonna hurt yourself."

They all watched as Henry sat up straight. He let out a long, squealing wheeze of smoke and doubled over in a fit of coughing. After several moments he regained composure and looked around at them all. Somebody grabbed the bong and passed it on.

"You okay?" the blonde girl asked him. She kissed him on the cheek again.

He gave a blank stare but then nodded. Time took on a new pace. Somebody turned up the music. A rap song raged. EPMD rapped "Strictly Business" with a riff from a Bob Marley song. Henry just sat there for a minute, watching the others nod their heads to the song. They mostly had their eyes closed. Marley sang the chorus.

Then, Henry jumped up so suddenly that everybody started and opened their eyes. In his eyes they saw what first appeared to be a frightened look. But, when Henry started laughing and doubled over, slapping his leg, they all erupted in laughter too. They kept their attention on him, as if he was going to put on a show. He started acting weird, gyrating his hips and almost dancing. His wild knee slammed the blonde girl in the back of the head. She let out a yelp and slapped his leg, but he didn't even notice. They all laughed at him again. As the laughter subsided Henry stopped moving and stood straight. They watched him as he searched the corners of the room, as if he was watching a fly buzz around. He stopped searching to listen to the music and then searched again.

"What are you doing, Kreiser?" Stanley asked. "You freaking out?"

Henry pointed at the ceiling. "Look!"

They all looked up.

"Did you see it?"

"Huh?" The blonde girl slapped his leg and pulled at it, trying to get him to sit down.

Henry shook his leg to get her hand off of it. "The music! The beat. You hear that beat? See it there? It's going up there. You see it?"

They laughed a little but then started looking at each other. "What's wrong with him?" one girl asked Stanley. Stanley got up and opened the window.

"Oh, my God!" Henry was dead serious. He pointed at the bed. "You see that!"

Paranoia suddenly struck all in the room. They grew quiet.

"What the fuck, Kreiser?" Stanley said.

"The snare drum. It's over there near the bed. See it?" Each time the snare sounded off, every fourth beat, he pointed over to the bed. And with every beat of the electronic drum, he pointed at the ceiling. "Listen. Watch." Henry started dancing as he pointed at the beats on the ceiling and the snares on the bed. "You see it. The beat is like a ball or something. It's fucking round, man. And the snare over here is, like, flat but breaking apart. It's sliding along the top of the fucking sheets."

Everybody stared at Henry blankly, not knowing what to say.

"Shut up!" Stanley yelled. "Just shut up!"

"No! I'm not gonna shut up." Henry leaped forward,

pointing at Stanley. "This is freakin' real, man, and you better realize it!"

"I'm going out to the keg," one of the girls said. She got up and left the room. One by one, the others also got up and left the room. As Stanley left, he smacked Henry in the back of the head. Henry swung around to hit him back, but he was much too slow. Stanley had left the room entirely by the time Henry's hand came around. Then, there was just Henry and the blonde girl. Henry continued to identify the shapes of the sounds as they moved from the speakers throughout the room. He watched them and pointed at them. He danced with them. She watched him for several minutes and then got up and grabbed his arms so he would stop. He pulled his arms away and continued to dance with the music.

"You're weird, Kreiser!" She hit stop on the stereo and left the room, slamming the door.

In the silence, Henry stopped dancing. He looked at the door and looked around the room. "Where'd they go?" He sat on the bed and then lay back. He heard a car running outside, as well as some people talking. The sound of the car rumbling mixed with the voices. He lay there, looking at the ceiling. "Where'd they fucking go?" It seemed like hours.

Stanley burst in, and Henry jumped suddenly off the bed.

"What are you doing?" Stanley grabbed Henry's shoulders. "Snap out of it."

"What?"

"Snap out of it!"

Henry drove home in a fog without the radio on. He listened to the sound of the car engine as he shifted gears. He took pleasure in making the engine race by leaving it in first gear. When he stopped at a traffic light, he pushed his eyelids open with his fingers.

Kate was awake when he got home. "Where were you?"

"You were where." Henry said.

"I asked a question."

"Question a asked I." Henry started laughing.

Kate grabbed his collar. "Sit down."

"Down sit." He sat.

"Have you been smoking pot?"

"Pot smoking been you have?" Henry doubled over in laughter. His keys dropped to the floor in front of him.

She picked them up and went into her bedroom.

"Hey Katesy! Katesy poo! Where you taking my keys?" He went to her door but it was shut so he went to bed.

Henry's body was heavy the next morning. He took long breaths. While not even fully awake, tears came to his eyes. He sobbed himself back to sleep and didn't wake until noon. When he did, he looked out at the daylight. He felt the moist pillowcase against his face. *I cried*, he thought. *I love her. Esther Sanchez. Esther. But she doesn't love me. Too young for her. Black curls. I kissed her lips. And she said she loves me. Oh, my God!* He sat up in bed suddenly. *What did I do with that blonde girl last night?*

He jumped out of bed and took a shower.

When he was ready to go, he couldn't find his keys. He took the cushions from the couch, reaching inside and looked underneath. He checked the kitchen drawers. He went up to the bedroom and searched the floor. He searched his pants pockets and then he went back downstairs.

Kate was there. "I took the keys."

"Why?"

"Because you drove stoned and probably drunk last night."

"I did *not*."

"Yes, Henry. You did! She gave the drugs to you, didn't she?"

"Who?"

"The Trenton girl," she said.

"No."

"But you did take drugs?"

He sat. "Yeah. I smoked pot."

"Well, you're not driving again until you turn eighteen.

And you're grounded for a month!"

"No! Not now. I need to go see Esther."

"No, you don't," she said. "I don't want you seeing her anymore anyway. She gave you drugs."

"I told you, she did not. I was at a party with my friends from school. I haven't seen Esther in two weeks."

"Well, you're not going anywhere for a month anyway," she declared. "Not her. Not your friends. Nowhere."

"I'm seventeen." He stood and poked his finger in the table.

"Precisely – you're still a child."

"No. I'm not. Can you give me my keys? I have to go."

"*Your* keys?"

"Yes, *my* keys."

"They're your brother's," she said, becoming agitated. "And I talked to him."

"What?"

"I talked to him. We agreed you don't need to use his car anymore."

"But he and I had an agreement," he argued. "It had nothing to do with you."

"That's where you're wrong, Henry. I'm your guardian. So everything you do has to do with me."

"How am I supposed to get to work and school?" He paced back and forth.

"Take the school bus! Maybe you'll go steady with a girl from around here who is your age." She watched him pace.

"I don't like these girls with their puffy hair!"

"It's not that you don't like them. It's that you don't want to be a normal kid."

"You want me to be normal?" he asked, getting louder.

"Yes!" she, too, got louder. "Be normal, for God's sakes."

"How can I be normal? I'm not like these other kids. Did I have a normal life?!"

"Don't ask stupid questions, Henry."

"Did I?"

"What makes you think anybody has a normal life?"

"Well, I don't know anybody who had a life like mine. Do you?"

"Yes! I do."

"Who?"

"Me!" She threw arms in the air, angrily. "You're so busy feeling sorry for yourself that you don't realize I went through the same thing."

"You were older. You didn't feel ... I was ..." He ran upstairs.

After Kate left that morning, Henry grabbed a ten-speed bike from the shed and took off. He rode to the Fotomat booth in the Fairless Hills Shopping Center.

Esther opened the window but didn't seem especially excited to see him.

"Why haven't you called me back?" he asked, out of breath and visibly upset.

"Been working a lot," she said.

"What time do you finish work?"

"Henry, listen—"

"Seven, right? I'll come back."

"Will you listen?" She grabbed for his arm but he dodged her.

"Yeah, we'll talk when I come back." He rode away.

At seven o'clock the blinds were pulled on the booth. He put the bike on the kickstand and knocked. She peeked out.

"Let me in," he said.

"I'm almost done," she called through the window.

"Come on. Let me in!"

She let him in. Cash was in piles. Photo envelopes filled a white canvas bag on the floor.

"Why haven't you called me back?"

"I told you. I've just been busy."

He kissed her. His sneak attack caught her off guard.

"What are you doing?" she asked.

"I love you, baby."

She laughed. "Henry." She kissed him back and they

held each other for several moments. She put her hands on his shoulders and squeezed. "You haven't been lifting, have you?"

"No. Why?"

"I can tell." She kissed him again.

He blushed at her comment. He pulled away but got a little rough. He saw their reflection in a small mirror on the wall. He watched the mirror as he turned her and pulled her skirt up. He looked at his coif and shook his head to fix it.

"Henry!"

He watched himself as if he was watching somebody else. He saw his arm in the mirror. It appeared skinny from that angle, so he flexed his bicep as he grabbed at her underwear.

"I said stop!" She smacked his hand away and slammed him back against the window, then pulled her skirt down. "Get out."

He froze.

"I said get out."

He went out and sat down on the curb.

When she came out of the booth, she walked over to a nearby bank and dropped a bag in a depository. She walked over to a bus stop as a bus approached.

He ran up to her before she got on.

"I'm sorry," he said.

"You're just a kid, Henry."

"No. I'm not. I'm a man now."

She stepped onto the bus and turned back. "Well, you have to start acting like a gentleman. Do you remember how to do that? Remember how nice you were?"

He shrugged. "Yes. Of course I do."

The bus driver sighed. "Let's go young lady!"

"Well," Esther continued, "when you're ready to treat me like a lady, give me a call. I was ready to let you back in, but then you act like an animal." She got on the bus and the door closed behind her.

He stood there for several minutes then got on his bike

and rode slowly away. He crossed the road to Lake Caroline. He sat on the picnic bench and watched the water.

When he got back home, Kate's car was in the driveway. She was on the phone.

"Come here, Henry," she called to him. She handed him the phone.

"Hello," Henry said into the receiver.

Byron was on the other end. "What are you doing?" Byron asked him.

"What do you mean?"

"I mean what the fuck are you doing? You drive my car stoned and drunk?"

"Sorry," Henry said into the receiver, glancing at Kate.

"Don't 'sorry' me," Byron said. "You're not using the car anymore."

"Why not?"

"Because you're an asshole, that's why. And you're an ungrateful bastard. Kate took you out of the Milt. She did you a huge favor. And this is what you do?"

"I didn't do anything wrong."

"And you won't even admit it?" Byron asked.

"No ... I didn't ... it was—"

"Henry!"

"I wasn't! I didn't—"

"Henry, will you listen to me?" Byron asked. "I have to tell you something."

"What?"

"You're going back to Hershey."

Henry looked over at Kate and then at the receiver. "No, I'm not," he said.

"Yes, you are. You're going back."

"No! I'm not!"

"Yes," Kate said as she got up and approached him. "You are. It's the best thing for you."

"Listen to me!" Henry yelled into the receiver and at Kate at the same time. "I have a girlfriend! She loves me! I love her. We make love! We're in fucking love. So I will not go anywhere I can't be close to her."

Kate welled up with tears but then shook them off. "Stop it, Henry. Just stop!"

"Yeah," Byron said, matching Henry's volume. "Yelling is not going to win the argument for you."

All three of them became quiet.

"So just let me be," Henry said into the receiver as he looked at Kate. "Okay?" He hung up, walked past Kate, and went upstairs.

Henry didn't sleep a wink. At four o'clock in the morning he packed a small bag; then quickly scribbled a note and left it on the coffee table.

> Kate, I'm sorry. I'm really sorry. I don't want to be a nuisance anymore. I need to go and do my own thing. I hope you understand.
> Love, Henry

In the brown bag that was tied to his handlebars, Henry had one pair of pants, two T-shirts, a pair of underwear and his contact lens container. The road back to Trenton was slick with pre-dawn dew. Early morning trucks began to appear. Henry rode into a small ditch and fell off the bike, trying to avoid a passing trash truck. Soon after he started again, another trash truck came hurtling down the road, so he stopped to watch it pass and turn into the trash dump up ahead. He could see a mountain of trash in the dawn light. One half was covered with a grassy meadow and a row of young trees, but the other half had a scar in the side of it. He watched trash trucks climb the high dump hill to the scar and drop their payload of garbage for the bulldozers to cover with dirt. As a truck moved in, thousands of seagulls twisted toward the sky. Then as the truck dumped, the seagulls swooped back down and engulfed the steaming pile in the scar. He watched the seagulls swoop up and down several times as the scar filled with trash.

Henry rode to Columbus Park and waited until Trenton woke up. When cars and passersby began to trickle by he went over to Esther's house. She answered the door in her pajamas. She looked at the bicycle and brown paper bag.

"What are you doing here?"

"I'm sorry about all that—lying to you and acting like a teenager." His eyes were tired and red.

"Okay."

"And I miss you."

"Okay." She shifted on her feet. "So?"

"And I'll try hard to treat you right."

"Okay. But why are you here right now? It's 7:00 in the morning."

"I left home, Esther. I need some place to go."

"You left home?!"

"Yeah. Things weren't working out."

"That's a big deal, Henry."

"So, can I stay here for a little?" he asked, reaching for her hand. "Until I find a place and I buy a car."

She took his hand. "I really think you should just go home now and fix whatever broke."

He turned away from her and sat on the step. "I can't. I'll explain it later, but I can't. If you don't want me to stay here, that's fine. I'll find a place."

She sat on the step next to him. "No, it's not that. I just want what's best for you."

He looked her in the eyes. "I really love you Esther."

She looped her arm in his. "I love you, too."

CHAPTER 10

Esther stayed home from work that day. They spent hours in bed getting familiar with each other again. She made iced tea in the afternoon, and Henry drank it all. When evening came, she went into the kitchen in her T-shirt and underwear. Henry heard the pots and pans. After a bit he smelled meat cooking. Then he heard Willy's voice, so he sat up in bed.

She ran into the bedroom.

"What are you doing out there in your underwear?" Henry put on a t-shirt.

"I didn't know Willy was gonna be here."

"Well, maybe you should wear pants when you go out there," he said.

She giggled as she pulled on her sweat pants. "You're jealous."

"No I'm not."

She jumped on the bed with him. She flicked his ear. "You're jealous, Henry."

"No, I'm not. I just think you should—"

"It's okay. It's kind of cute," she said. She went back out to the kitchen.

Henry followed her out to the kitchen and helped her finish cooking dinner. He made garlic bread with butter in the toaster oven.

Willy came in and sat down at the kitchen table.

"How about you set the table?" Esther asked Willy.

"Do what?" Willy slouched down in the chair.

"Set out the plates and silverware."

Willy sat there for several seconds, then got up and set the table.

When they sat down to eat, Henry didn't lift his head until he was through with two platefuls.

"You should breathe," Willy said.

Henry chewed his last bite and swallowed it. He took a drink of water. "Thanks."

"Don't thank me. Just learn to calm the fuck down."

Henry glanced at Esther then back at Willy. "What are you talkin' about? How am I not calm?" Henry asked.

"I'll tell you in time."

"I wish you would tell me now because—"

"Don't challenge me motherfucker," Willy said, calmly.

Esther slammed her fork down. "Willy!"

After dinner Henry fell asleep for an hour. When he woke up Esther was folding laundry and putting it in the dresser. Henry sat up. "This is an amazing day for me. You realize that Esther?"

She turned and searched his eyes. "Why?"

"Because I declared my independence and I'm getting a fresh start."

"But, your independence came at your sister's expense—don't you think?"

"I don't think so. I'm not happy about the way it turned out. But I'm sure she'll eventually see that this is what I needed to do. This is bigger than that, though."

"How so?" She folded a pair of his underwear and put them in the drawer with hers.

"It's what I always wanted and needed—ever since I was at Milton Hershey. And now that I've taken this step I want to... I think we should..."

"Go ahead," she said, closing a drawer and sitting back on the bed with him.

"Well, on the phone last month you mentioned we could have a good life together. I know right now I'm only staying here temporarily but I think we should think about how we can do that."

"When I said that, my point was that you were too young. I was saying we could have had a good life together... *if you were older.*"

He looked out the window through the clear plastic that covered it. He nodded. "I'm seventeen and have a job. That's not so bad, is it?"

"But, I want you to finish school," she said. "One more year and you have a high school diploma. Then maybe we can talk about having a life together."

Henry thought about her statement for a long moment, and then got out of bed and tugged on the plastic on the window. He pulled out one of the staples that was holding the plastic in place. "It's almost summer," he said. "Maybe we can take the plastic off and let some fresh air in."

"That would be nice," she said. "I've been meaning to do some things around the house this week."

He thought for a moment. "Do you have a pen and paper?"

"In the top drawer next to the stove. Why?"

That evening Henry walked around the house making a list: remove plastic from bedroom windows, fresh coat of paint on kitchen wall, tighten front door lock. When he went into the living room Willy was sitting with his legs up on the coffee table, blocking Henry from passing.

"Can I get by?" Henry asked.

Willy slowly moved one leg, then the other. At the living room window Henry jotted another note on the paper: caulk needed to prevent further leaks.

"What're you doin?" Willy asked.

"I'm writin' down some notes of things that need to be fixed around here."

"What, you suddenly the super?"

"I'm gonna be stayin' here for a little bit so just want to... you know..."

"You know what's wrong with you?" Willy asked, putting his feet back up on the coffee table.

Henry rolled his eyes. "What's wrong with me, Willy?"

"You got a baby face. And you seem like ... I don't know ... you seem ..." He looked at the ceiling, searching for the right word. "You seem like you ain't got no direction."

Henry laughed uncomfortably.

"Don't laugh. I'm serious." Willy showed his gold tooth in a sarcastic semi-smile. "Why you gonna fuck around tryin' to fix things that ain't broke?"

Henry stepped to leave, but Willy's legs blocked his exit. "You wanna leave me the fuck alone?"

"Sit the fuck down," Willy said. "I'm here to help you."

Henry sat. "Help me what?"

"Help you get a direction in life."

"Thanks, but I have all the direction I need."

"Where you goin' then? I mean in your life. Tell me. What are you gonna do? You're seventeen now."

Henry shrugged. "I work at the bingo chip factory. I'm operating a machine, so I think I'll work there."

"How you gonna make any money at a factory? You do wanna make money, right?"

"Hell yeah! I want to make lots of money."

Willy nodded. "Well, you ain't gonna make no money at a factory."

"Well, if I own the factory I will."

"Don't be a dumbass, man," Willy paused for a second. He softened his tone. "Let's you and me take a walk."

"Where to?"

"Down the street. Let's talk about making money."

"Nah. Thanks. I'm gonna hang here. I wanna get this list done."

* * *

Each weekday Henry rode the bicycle from Trenton to school and work in Levittown. It took an hour and a half each way. On the days he worked, he got back home to Esther late in the evening. The long rides gave him plenty of time to think, and the physical exertion meant solid nights of sleep. Within a month and a half of moving in with Esther, he finished eleventh grade.

Summer vacation allowed Henry more free time, so he decided to make the repairs he had written down. He gave the kitchen a fresh coat of tan paint. He pulled the plastic from the bedroom windows, folded it up, and tucked it under the bed. He tightened the lock on the front door and neatly caulked the living room window.

One night, Henry woke up as Esther got out of bed. Light flooded into the dark room as she went out and closed the door. Then, he heard her in the kitchen talking to Ms. Sanchez, who had just gotten home from work.

"The wall is beautiful," he heard Ms. Sanchez say.

Henry smiled to himself.

"He fixed the front door and pulled the plastic off the windows too," Esther told her mother. Then, they began speaking in hushed tones and Henry could no longer make out the words.

After the toilet flushed and Esther came back into the bedroom, she slipped under the sheet, pulled Henry close, and held him tight. He pretended he was sleeping and acted groggy, as he turned, wrapped his arms around her, and tangled his legs with hers. He put his lips on her forehead.

"You awake?" she asked.

"Umm. Huh?"

"You're not awake are you?"

"Now, I am," he said. He put his nose against hers.

"My mom really likes you," Esther whispered, "and she understands you need a place to stay. So, there's no rush for you to move out, at least not right now."

He was speechless. He was relieved and happy. He held her tightly.

In the morning, he sat on the bed as she put her makeup on in the dresser mirror.

"I'd like to continue what I already started," he declared.

"What do you mean?" She carefully applied blue eyeliner.

"I mean in helping around the house—and making this a better place."

"Great!" she said.

"But I was wondering if..." He paused and thought to

himself for a moment.

"What?" She turned to him.

"What do you think Willy's gonna do?"

"What do you mean?"

"I mean, you know, I'm seventeen and I moved on in my life to something new. Like, I think seventeen is a good time for a guy to go out into the world."

"Oh." She sat on the bed next to him. "You don't like him do you?"

"Ah, nah," he waved it off nonchalantly. "I do. It's not that. I just want him to do what's best for him."

"What's best for him?" she asked. "I don't think he's really in a good position to do anything, so I think to stay here for now is the best thing for him." She stood up to the mirror again and began applying lipstick.

"Yeah. I guess."

"You don't feel threatened by him, do you?" She looked at him in the mirror.

"Threatened? No." He laughed—a bit forced. "Of course not."

After finishing the repairs at the house, Henry had more idle time. So, on the days he didn't work at the factory, he wandered around the neighborhood. Chambersburg was split by Hamilton Avenue. One side of the avenue was predominantly Italian-American—bakeries and row-homes with faux Italianate fronts—and the other side was a Latin neighborhood with bodegas and smaller row-homes.

One day Henry spotted Willy walking through Columbus Park. An orange, early-seventies style Toyota with tinted windows pulled up on Hamilton Avenue and honked its horn to get Willy's attention. It stopped. A beat thumped with bass from the inside. Henry sat on a bench and watched. The driver opened his door and the music spilled out—a fast dance rhythm with the thump of the beat. Two Latin girls got out of the passenger side. When Henry saw the girls step into his view, he leaned forward to take a closer look. Their hair was pulled back tightly and they both wore several gold earrings. Snug jeans revealed shapely legs and Wigwams were bunched around their ankles. Willy shook hands and knocked shoulders with the driver, then leaned against the car. The girls kissed Willy on the cheek and hung on his shoulders affectionately. Henry was intrigued—the girls, the car, the music. He wanted a closer look, so he walked in their direction even though there was no clear reason for him to go that way. He crossed through a flower bed and jumped over a park bench. When he walked by, he glanced over at them multiple times—trying to make eye contact with Willy. But Willy didn't see Henry, and the car's driver did. And, when Henry glanced over again, the driver gave Henry a nasty stare. Henry walked on.

One evening that week Esther worked late, so Henry made himself a pot of spaghetti and meatballs with *Ragu* tomato sauce. When finished eating, he placed the remaining spaghetti and meatballs neatly on a plate. Just as he was wrapping it in plastic wrap, Willy walked in.

"That for me?" Willy asked. He sat down at the kitchen table.

"Uh... it's for Esther actually."

Willy looked at the plate and nodded. Henry put it in the refrigerator.

"Usually she makes enough for me," Willy said.

"Oh, sorry. Tonight I cooked."

"So, then who ate my portion?" Willy asked.

Henry sighed. He went to the refrigerator and pulled out the plate. He placed it on the table in front of Willy then grabbed a fork and a knife from a drawer and laid them nicely next to the plate. "Your dinner, sir," Henry said as he held a napkin out for Willy.

Willy stared at the napkin for a second then took it. He started laughing.

"Why you laughin'?" Henry asked.

"Just laughin'. Don't make nothin' out of it."

Henry slouched down in the chair across the table as Willy began to eat.

After a few minutes Henry straightened up in the

chair. "What's your deal Willy?"

"What do you mean?"

"I mean how'd you end up here?"

"That's my business, isn't it?"

Henry grew quiet and slouched back down as Willy ate.

"This spaghetti is pretty fuckin' good," Willy said. "Better than Esther's."

"Don't tell her." Henry lowered his voice and looked over his shoulder, pretending he had reason to be sneaky. "But I dumped all the grated cheese in there. That's why it's so good."

Willy laughed. "Well I just got rid of the evidence brotha. So, no worries." He got up, took his plate to the sink. As he was leaving the room Willy stopped and stood in front of Henry. "Wanna know my deal?" Willy asked.

"Huh?"

"You asked what my deal was."

"Yeah. Tell me," Henry said.

"My parents drank a lot. My Dad always beat my Mom. My Mom always beat me. Then, one day she shot my Dad in the leg. When he got back from the hospital a few days later he took the gun and shot a clerk in a store down the street. He's been in jail since. Child services took custody of me because they didn't like my mom. I went into foster homes—one after the next. Then I committed a couple little crimes and got locked up in juvy for a year before coming here. Now I'm reformed." He winked at Henry and walked out.

Henry didn't know how to respond. He sat up in his chair as he watched Willy walk down the hall to the living room. *Fuck,* he thought. *That's fucked the fuck up.* He went to the sink and washed Willy's plate and silverware.

Later that week, at a corner store, Henry picked up an *Auto Shopper* magazine. In the evening he sat in bed and perused the car ads while Esther finished the dishes. Endless junkers cried 'dependable,' but he wasn't interested. She came in and sat next to him. "I like this one," he told her, pointing to a sporty seventies Toyota with tinted windows and chrome rims.

"That's a thousand dollars," she said. "How much do you have?"

"I have one thousand four hundred," he said proudly.

"Maybe you should buy a cheaper car and save the rest, just in case."

"Just in case what?" He put the *Auto Shopper* down.

"Well, I was thinking..." she said. "I was thinking maybe you could... I don't mean to ask for money but maybe you can contribute a few dollars here and there for rent."

"Oh. Esther, I'm sorry. I completely forgot. I was going to offer to pay some money."

"No problem," she said, sincerely. "Sorry I had to bring it up." She picked up the magazine and began thumbing through it. "What about this one? Six hundred dollars."

He examined the ad. It was a long, white, four-door car. "*What?* I'm not driving around in that thing. I'll look like a grandmom."

"It's a more practical car than the one you're looking at. And it's newer so it should last longer too."

"I don't know." He flipped through the pages to the other ad. "The Toyota looks newer to me. See how shiny it is," he said, touching the ad.

Henry went out to the living room. "Hey man," he said to Willy, who was watching T.V.

Willy nodded without turning to Henry.

"Hey man," Henry said again, holding out the *Auto Shopper* magazine this time. "I'm gonna get this car and maybe we can cruise around and stuff."

Willy looked at the ad while Henry held it. "Really?!" Willy asked. "That's a nice fuckin' car!"

"Yeah," Henry looked at the ad again. "I think I'm gonna buy it tomorrow."

"Damn motherfucker!" Willy jumped up and extended his hand to Henry. "I like how you operate."

They shook hands.

Henry woke up several times throughout the night, imagining himself driving the Toyota through Trenton. He pictured himself pulling up at Columbus Park with Esther and picking up Willy. He imagined letting other Latin girls in tight jeans and Wigwams slide in the back with Esther. They all laughed and danced and bounced around to the fast dance rhythm and heavy beat as Henry sped through the streets of Trenton.

In the morning, he called the number in the Toyota ad and made an appointment. Later that day he went to Center Street to see it—on a long block lined with rows of homes. The car wasn't as shiny as it seemed in the picture, and there were a couple spots where the paint was chipped. But it was spotless inside and out, and had three "Vanillaroma" air freshener trees hanging from the mirror. A Puerto Rican flag hung there too.

"I'll remove the flag," the guy said.

"Nah. That's cool." Henry reached inside the car and touched the tinted window in the back. "You install the tinting?"

"Professionally installed." The guy opened the back door. A large speaker lay across the seat. "Kicker" was written on it in block letters.

"Whoa." Henry ran his hand over it. "I bet that kicks the fucking beats."

"Oh, I should have told you, the Kicker doesn't come with the car."

"Okay. Can I hear it anyway?"

The guy got in the driver's seat and turned on the stereo. It was the same fast rhythm and dance beat Henry heard before. A man sang passionately.

Henry immediately felt the music move him. "Who's this?" he asked.

"Stevie B."

"Oh yeah. Freestyle, right?"

"Exactly."

"My girlfriend is half Puerto Rican ... so ... you know ... I know ..."

"You know... what?" the guy asked.

"I meant... oh ... nothing. Can you turn it up?"

When the guy turned up the music, the speaker in the

backseat boomed and the world around them stopped. A man on the street stopped to take a look, and cars slowed down as they passed by. Henry saw all the attention the car was getting. He made some muted dance moves for a few beats.

Then, the guy turned down the stereo. "As I said, the Kicker's not for sale. It's going in my new car."

"Come on, man. How much you want for it?"

"No. Sorry bro."

"I'll make it worth your while." Henry said, rubbing his fingers together to indicate cash.

"You really want it, don't you?"

"Yeah. Hell, yeah. It belongs in this car."

"Three hundred," the guy offered.

"How about two hundred?"

"Deal!" He patted Henry on the back. "Twelve hundred dollars for the whole package!"

"Can I have the Stevie B. tape?"

"I'll throw it in for thirty more!"

When Henry was a block away from home, Esther heard the thump of the bass. As it got closer, she heard the rhythm and the words. Stevie B. sang "Diamond Girl." She heard the horn honk but didn't realize who it was. When she heard it a second time she ran to the window. Henry was standing next to the car with a big smile on his face.

"What do you think?" he called up to her.

Willy came to the other window. "Nice!"

Esther laughed and shook her head.

Later, while sitting in the passenger seat, Esther took the Puerto Rican flag off the rearview mirror. "It's funny seeing you in this car," she said.

"What do you mean?"

"I just mean it's strange for me. I picture you in like, a different car—maybe a truck."

He laughed. "Oh, like I'm a country boy or something?" Henry pulled the rearview mirror toward his face and tried to imagine what he looked like sitting in his new car. He played with his hair.

Then, Willy popped his face in the driver's side

window, startling both of them. "You the man, Kreiser," he said. He extended his hand to Henry. They shook.

Henry spent the afternoon and evening primping the car. He polished the dashboard with 'Armor All', and then buffed the rims. He was locking the car just after dark when Willy came out.

"Come with me," Willy said to Henry.

"Where to?"

"Just come with me. Let's take a walk—talk about making money."

"All right. Let's talk."

He locked the car and they began to walk away when they both heard the second floor window open. They looked up and saw Esther pop her head out.

"Where you going?" she called down to Henry.

"Me and Willy gonna take a walk."

"Hold on. I need to talk to you."

Willy shook his head. "Come on, Henry. Don't wait for her."

"Hold on. She's coming down."

She came out a few moments later and approached Henry while Willy stood back. "Come here a second," she whispered, pulling Henry aside further.

Henry stepped aside with her. "What?"

"Why are you talking like that?" she asked.

"Like what?"

"Like Willy. You said, 'we gonna take a walk'."

"What? No, I didn't."

"Ok. Whatever. Why don't you come inside, though?" She took his hand in hers. "We'll watch a movie."

Henry looked over at Willy. "Hey Will. I'm gonna head in. Talk to you later."

"What!? Come here." Willy called him over.

Henry looked at Esther and rolled his eyes. He approached Willy.

"What are you doin'?" Willy asked, lowering his voice.

"I'm gonna hang with my girl."

"Don't do that, dumbass."

"What!?" Henry asked, defensively.

"Don't just go when she tells you. You'll get no respect."

"Ah, man," Henry said. "Whatever."

"I'm fuckin' serious. Come with me."

"All, right. Just for a minute, though." Henry turned back to Esther. "I'm gonna be back in a minute. We gonna take a walk to talk guy stuff."

"Fine." She went inside.

Willy and Henry walked through Columbus Park. "I see a lot of potential in you, Kreiser," Willy said. A mild fog gathered the light from the streetlights, leaving stretches of dark in between. Willy was small and skinny but had a hefty strut. His eyes were steady and straight under his bandanna. His arms swung slowly and bounced on every other step. He hacked and spit a bullet.

Henry spit too, but it sprayed.

Willy stopped and grabbed Henry's arm. "That's what's wrong with you."

"What?"

"Whatever you just did."

"Spit?"

"That isn't how you spit!" Willy let go of Henry's arm.

"Oh. You're gonna teach me how to spit now?"

"Yeah!"

"Yeah?"

"Come here into the light." Willy walked over to stand below a streetlight. Henry followed. "You don't spray your saliva all over the place," Willy said. "You fuckin' shoot it out. The purpose of spitting is to get the saliva out of your mouth and on the ground, not all over your chin." Willy hacked some saliva and spat. It hit the ground like a bullet. "Like that."

Henry tried the same. But again he sprayed.

"No! No. No. Use your head to give it momentum—like you're head-butting somebody. And your mouth has to be shaped like the barrel of a gun shooting the bullet."

Henry tried again. He knocked his head quickly when he spat, and he clenched his lips into the shape of cylinder, but the timing was off and the spit dribbled onto his chin.

He wiped it with his sleeve and laughed. "Duh," he said.

"Don't laugh. What the fuck are you laughing for? I can't believe you're seventeen and nobody ever taught you this shit."

"Ah, come on, man. We gonna take a walk or what?" Henry started walking again.

"This way." Willy led him down Hamilton Avenue. Then they went down Hudson Street over to Tyler Street. They stopped at the corner, looking at a row of homes, most of which were boarded up. Tyler Street was especially dark and full of trash.

"What do you see here?" Willy asked.

"I see a bunch of shitty houses."

"Exactly. And what else?"

"Uh... some trash?"

"No. See, you're missing something. Like I was saying before, I see a lot of potential in you. But you're not there yet. Got no precision in yo vision."

A boy in a hooded sweatshirt moved in the dark behind them quickly, startling Henry. Willy spun around and pulled the boy aside in one quick movement. He yanked the boy's hood even further down over his face, whispered something in his ear, and then pushed him back on his way. Willy sighed as he returned to Henry's side.

"Who was that?" Henry asked.

"Let's go," Willy said, ignoring Henry's question.

They went into the Trenton Train Station. They sat on fixed plastic chairs in front of the board listing arrivals and departures.

"You understand life is unfair, right?"

"Yeah. Really fucking unfair."

"Right, and some people are born into a life where they have everything they need. And others are born into a world of shit."

Henry nodded his head. He looked at the board. It was flipping through destinations and arrivals now: Boston, New York, Philadelphia, Baltimore, Miami.

"So what is a person to do—I mean, a person who is

born into the world of shit?"

"I don't know." Henry was still looking at the board.

Willy grabbed his arm. "Pay attention!"

Henry was startled and a little scared at the sudden aggression and anger in Willy's eyes.

"People born into the shit have the right to take things from people born with everything. That's how we rebalance."

Henry shook his arm free. "Don't touch my fucking arm. I wasn't born with everything!"

"I know you weren't, asshole. Esther told me your story."

"She did?"

"Yeah," Willy said. "It's fucked up."

"So, what's your point?"

"It's about your potential. You know when I first met you I was thinking this dude is a corny ass white dude from the suburbs. But in just a few months I see that you've come a long way."

"Thanks." Henry gave a half smile. "I think."

"Yeah, I'm giving you a compliment. But also telling you; you have further to go."

"I'm fine with where I am."

"You think you there, but you not there. You got it on the inside, but not on the outside. Again, that comes from a lack of precision in yo vision." Willy turned to the arrivals and destinations board. He held his hands out and framed the board with his fingers for Henry. "What happens next in the movie of Henry Kreiser's life? Where are we at in that movie? How does it end? Those are the questions you gotta ask yourself."

Henry looked through Willy's fingers at the board. It started flipping through the cities again. Henry laughed.

"Don't laugh Kreiser. You gotta figure out how to be the star of your movie. If you don't, it's not gonna end the way you want it to."

Henry laughed. "You got a strange way of looking at things." He got up. "I'm goin' back to the house."

In the bedroom that evening, Esther tied her hair back

as she prepared for bed. She looked at Henry in the mirror. He was standing in front of the closet, looking through his clothes—just a few items on hangers.

"I don't have to worry about you, do I?" she asked.

He pulled out a t-shirt with a surfer and wave design on the front of it. "No... what do you mean?"

She turned toward him and looked at the t-shirt in his hand. "Well, I hope you don't start hanging out with Willy too much."

"Oh. Yeah." He pulled out another t-shirt. "Sorry about taking off with him before. He's just so pushy."

"You should just tell him no," she said.

He shrugged. "I need some new clothes."

"So, let's go shopping this weekend," she said. "But, listen, I think you should stand up to him and say no when he pressures you."

"He doesn't pressure me," he said, taking a serious tone. "And I can handle it."

He continued looking through his clothes as she watched.

"I was thinking about your idea," she said, "that it might be a good time in Willy's life—being seventeen—for him to move on. I think I might ask my mom to have a talk with him."

"Really?" He turned to her. "Why?"

"Because I think it's a good time."

"I don't know. I would just leave him alone for now."

"You're the one who had the idea in the first place," she argued, quietly.

"I know," he said. "But, as I get to know him I realize it's probably not a good time for him to leave."

That weekend Henry walked with Esther through the business district on South Broad Street in Trenton. They passed a diner and a record shop, and he bought new high-top basketball sneakers at a sporting goods store. They stopped in front of a barber shop with Puerto Rican flags in the window and chairs that were filled with Latino men. Henry watched one man leave the shop with a closely cropped cut. Then he took a close look at a picture in the window of a man with the same style haircut. Henry looked at his own reflection in the window and ran his fingers through his permed coif. He turned to Esther. "You see? That's my problem."

"What?"

"My hair. I got this big poof on top of my head."

"But your hair is just like the ones in the picture here." She pointed at the picture.

"No, it's not. Mine is much higher on top. It's a curly poof up there. And it's not as short on the sides and back."

"Yeah, it's a little different, I guess. But I like it."

"It's fine for Levittown. But if I'm gonna hang around Trenton, it should be tight, like these guys."

"Don't be silly. Don't try to change who you are." She grabbed his arm. "Let's go."

"I'm not talking about changing me. I'm just talking about looking like … you know."

"Like what?"

"Like I'm from here."

"But you're not from here." She tugged at his arm. "Come on!"

They went home.

A few days later, Henry couldn't find a parking spot on his block, so he parked his car a couple blocks away from home—across Hamilton Avenue in the Latin neighborhood. Walking back to the house he happened upon a group of teenagers that were milling around a stoop with a boom box. He sensed immediately that they began talking about him, so, without thinking about it, he put a bit of a swagger in his step. Feeling hostility, he avoided eye contact as he swaggered past. The group became quiet. And, as Henry walked on, he figured he had been unnecessarily self-conscious. A sense of relief set in and he began walking without the swagger again. But then, the group burst into laughter. When Henry stopped and turned to look back they all stopped laughing and stared at him. One guy, wearing a red bandanna, stepped toward Henry and nodded in an unfriendly way. Henry left immediately.

Later that day, Henry stood in the mirror, looking at his high curly coif. He ran his fingers through it and examined it from several different angles, hoping he would find a way to appreciate it as he had in the past. But, the more he looked at it the more he hated it. He especially hated the curls. *I gotta cut it*, he decided. Then, he searched around bathroom and opened the cabinet under the sink, where he found what he was looking for—a pair of scissors and electric clippers.

When he started clipping, he took a swipe at the side of his head. A clump of hair fell on his shoulder and he paused for a second, looking at it. Then he started in earnest, taking wild swipes at the side and back of his head and buzzing his hair down to the skin. Within minutes he was practically bald all the way around the sides and back of his head. He focused on his coif now. And he moved toward it with the clippers several times. But he couldn't bring himself to touch it, so he put the clippers down. He started on the top with the scissors, taking small chunks of hair off with each snip. He continued that way, slowly sculpting the top and removing the curls, but otherwise leaving the coif in place. Twenty minutes after he started, Henry set the scissors down and examined his new haircut. It was a tall, boxy flattop now and it excited him to just stand there and behold it. He looked at himself from every angle for several minutes. He made tough guy faces. Then, he ran out of the house.

When Henry entered the apartment that evening, Esther stood at the top of the steps looking down at him. She barely recognized him at first glance. "Oh, my God."

Besides his new, closely cropped, tall flat-top, he also had a bandanna around his forehead, just above his eyebrows. And a gold cross on a thick gold chain hung down to his belly.

"What on earth happened to you?" She was shocked.

"What?" He walked up the steps, a little uncomfortable in his skin but otherwise proud.

"Your haircut... what happened? The bandanna? The necklace? I didn't know you wanted to change your whole look."

Willy was in the living room. He jumped up from the couch. "Yo! Kreiser!"

"Hey, man." Henry responded, tapping the gold cross.

"Lookin' good, my brotha. That's what I'm talking about. Now you look like a dude with precision in his vision."

"Thanks, brotha."

Willy leaned into him. "You might wanna take the top down a notch or two, though," he advised quietly. "And you fucked it up in the back a little bit."

"Nah, it's cool," Henry said. "I like it like this."

Esther watched. "Why did you—"

"I just needed some change," Henry said.

"Yeah," Willy said. "He just needed some change. Don't give him a hard time."

"I didn't," she said, defensively. "I wasn't. I was just asking him. Can't I ask my boyfriend?"

"Well, I know what you're drivin' at, Esther," Willy said. "You want him to be a little white boy."

"But... he *is* white. Isn't he?" Esther walked out.

"No, I'm not." Henry called after her. He followed her to the bedroom.

"I have to go to bed." She took off her pants and looked at him. "You're not white?" She laughed and grabbed his hand.

"I'm not white like that, I mean," Henry explained. "Like he means. That's what I mean. Why you laughin'?"

She struggled to stop laughing. "I'm not. Let's go to bed."

He kneeled on the bed and looked in the mirror at himself. "You like it?"

She shrugged. "It's okay."

"Well, come here." He lay across the bed, fixing his gold chain so it was visible to her. "Come here. Show me you like my new look."

"Sure. It's cute I guess," she said. She got in bed, slipping under the covers.

"I can tell you don't like it," he said. He stayed on top

of the covers. She soon fell asleep. He fixed his chain and lay there picturing himself walking down the sidewalk through a crowd of people. *That's right, motherfuckers,* he thought. *Henry fuckin' Kreiser. In your fuckin face!* He fell asleep with his clothes on, clutching the gold cross.

When Henry drove his car he felt complete. His hair and clothes, the car and music, got him exactly the looks he wanted—especially in Pennsylvania.

A few weeks later on an August afternoon, he turned onto Hanford Street, to go to the bingo chip factory. His music was so loud and his tinted windows so dark that he didn't notice he nearly ran another car, a Jaguar, off the road. But the driver of the Jaguar honked to let him know. Curious as to who was honking, Henry rolled down his window and looked in his side-view mirror. He saw the bumper and side of the Jaguar but couldn't see the driver. Annoyed that somebody was honking at him—somebody in a luxury car no less—Henry slowed down even more. When the Jaguar tried to pass him, Henry swerved to block it. Finally, the driver of the other car hit the gas hard and held the horn at the same time. Henry was provoked. *Asshole,* he thought. As the car sped past and the driver looked over at him, Henry pointed his fingers in the shape of pistol and pulled the imaginary trigger. But, much to his surprise, at the very same moment he realized the driver was Mr. Penn—his boss.

Fuck, Henry thought, pulling his hand down. He turned down the volume and continued to the factory. He quietly went into work.

When Henry was tending to a machine an hour later, Mr. Penn approached him. Beside Mr. Penn was the factory supervisor.

Henry turned off the machine.

"Do you mind coming to the office?" Mr. Penn asked.

Henry went into the office with him while the supervisor stood outside of the door.

"Henry. What did I tell you about wearing the bandanna and gold chain while working?"

"You said not to wear them."

"And why did I tell you that?"

"For safety."

"Right, then why are you still wearing them?"

Henry shifted on his feet and glanced out the window. He shrugged.

"I'm afraid, we're going to have to let you go, Henry."

"*What?!*" Henry pushed his bandanna up a little off his eyes. "Why?"

Mr. Penn sat down in his chair and leaned back. "People and companies grow and change. Companies change by adapting to the dynamic needs of their customers. But people change based on the shifting path to their future."

"I... I'm sorry. I don't know what you mean."

"Your attitude has changed in a way that I don't think is consistent with the values of this company." Mr. Penn pointed to Henry's clothing.

"Oh." Henry looked down at himself. "That's what this is about? I'll take them off. I'm sorry, I just forgot."

Mr. Penn shook his head. "No. *I'm* Sorry, Henry. There are broader problems with you lately that I don't think are easily resolved."

"I've been coming to work and doing my job," Henry protested.

"Yes. But you've been late several times, including today. And you're outwardly a very different person then you were even just a month ago. I just don't think you are a good fit for the company anymore."

"Really? So this is it?"

"I'm afraid it is." Mr. Penn handed Henry a bank envelope. "Your last paycheck," he said.

Henry stuffed the envelope in his pocket, turned his head down and walked out.

When Henry got back to Trenton and parked his car, he saw the light on in the living room, so he didn't go into the apartment. Instead he walked into Columbus Park and thought about his predicament. He counted the money in the envelope, then hacked and spit with ease and precision. It hit the pavement like a bullet.

"Good work," somebody called from across the street.

Henry saw Willy crossing over toward him.

"I was watching you Kreiser. It's all coming together."

"Huh?"

"You were walking like a fuckin beast man. You don't understand, when I looked over at you I saw a bad-ass motherfucker."

"Shut-up."

"No really. Then you spit. It was perfect."

Henry laughed, but it wasn't an uncomfortable loose laugh. It was tight and full of confidence. His serious eyes shot over at Willy. Henry walked away.

Willy caught up with him. He nudged him with his elbow. "Come on," Willy said.

"What? Where?"

"Come with me. Let's talk about making money."

"Nah. I'm gonna go in. I gotta talk to Esther."

"Do that later man. I got an idea. Come on!"

They walked off together. They turned onto Tyler Street; then went down a dark alley between two rundown buildings.

"Where we goin'?" Henry asked.

"Just come on and shut-up."

They entered the backyard of one of the buildings. Henry watched Willy go to a backdoor that was boarded up, and remove a two-by-four that was lying across the door. Willy reached behind a piece of plywood and unlatched something. He shook it a few times; then it swung open.

Willy flicked on a light—just a bulb on the ceiling. They entered squalor. There was no furniture in the first room— the kitchen. Willy pulled the door shut and they walked through the kitchen into a middle room. He flicked on another light. There was a mattress on the floor with a filthy sheet across it. A wooden chair was in the corner, and there were vials and plastic bags all over the floor between it and the mattress.

"Wow," Henry said, "whose house is this?"

Willy's back was to Henry. Henry waited for an answer, but Willy said nothing.

"Hey, whose house is this?"

Willy swung around so quickly that Henry didn't know what was coming. He didn't even have time to move or block. And Willy's fist slammed into Henry's temple. Henry was knocked back several steps and he dropped onto one knee. He was dazed and it took him a few seconds to regain balance and stand up. When he did, he saw Willy standing in front of him.

"You see. You always gotta be prepared for..."

Henry struck back suddenly, slamming his fist into Willy's cheek. Willy lost footing for a second, then Henry rushed forward.

"Yo!" Willy yelled, putting his hand up.

Henry stopped. "Why the fuck did you do that?" he asked.

"I just wanted to see who you were."

Henry sat down on the chair and rubbed his temple. A red mark was turning into a lump. Willy held his cheek. He spat out some blood on the floor.

"Well," Henry said, "you know I'm twenty pounds heavier than you and five inches taller, so you might want to think twice next time."

"My brotha," Willy pulled his pistol from his waistband and tossed it on the bed. "That's what I've been trying to tell you. Your size ain't gonna make a difference. It's your vision and determination that will—and it is starting to make the difference."

"Whatever." Henry stared at the gun on the bed. "What... what kind of gun is it?"

"It shoots bullets."

"Ha ha. Funny. I mean, what caliber is it?"

"It's a nine dude." Willy sat on the bed and looked at Henry dead in the eyes. "Listen man, I want you to work with me," he said.

"Huh?"

"Next week I'm getting an opportunity. This house is gonna be the center of it all."

"This house? What are you talking about?"

"You ain't figured it out yet? You that dense?"

"No. I know. You're dealin' something, right?"

Willy nodded. "Very good Kreiser. I got the sellers all worked out for this neighborhood. But I need somebody to take me for my weekly pick-up in West Trenton—somebody inconspicuous—like you white boy—that has a car—like you."

Henry thought about it. "Oh. That's what you've wanted to talk to me about. You think I'm gonna become a drug dealer all of a sudden. Ha! Nah, thanks anyway."

Henry got up from the chair to leave but Willy grabbed his arm. "Come on Kreiser."

"No. Sorry." Henry peeled Willy's hand off and left the house.

Near bedtime Henry and Esther were squeezed into the bathroom. "He's just a product of his circumstances," Henry said. "I mean, how he acts and talks and even how he dresses."

"What do you mean?" She began washing her face.

"I mean, he knows what he wants, and everything he does is for that."

"What does he want?"

"That doesn't matter. He's the one who has to know that, not us. We only have to know what *we* want."

"You're not making sense, Henry." She dried her face with a towel. "What are you talking about?"

"I'm talking about heading for a destination. He says 'precision in your vision'. That means something."

"Huh?!"

"I gotta lot of respect for that dude because he has a vision of where he wants to go."

"*Respect?* He's seventeen, like you, but he dropped out of school and doesn't even have a job. What do you respect about that?"

"Yeah, but he comes from a different set of circumstances than me. So, I *do* have respect for him because he's doin' pretty good with the cards he's been dealt in life."

"Maybe," she said. "But you're a much better, more responsible person than he is."

"That's what I want to tell you," Henry said. "About my job."

She was distracted from their conversation suddenly, looking in the mirror at Henry's head where Willy had hit him. There was a black and blue lump. "What happened?"

"I bumped into the freakin door," he said. "Such a clutz."

She touched it. "We should put ice on it."

That evening Henry never got the opportunity to tell her he no longer had a job. He left in the following morning as if he was going to work but instead went job searching. When Esther wasn't home, he scanned the help-wanted section of the *Trentonian* newspaper. He made some calls and got some bites. He went to a grocery store on Hamilton Avenue to fill out an application. But the store manager looked at Henry from sneakers to bandanna and returned to gaze at the thick gold chain. He glanced at Henry's application. "Sorry," the manager said. "The position has been filled."

Henry drove around Trenton, crossed over the river to Bucks County. He applied to multiple jobs but most employers made their decision before Henry even began filling out the application.

Later that week when he left the house in Trenton, he noticed that a car was following him. He made an odd turn to confirm, and it still followed. Then he drove fast, darting through some back streets, and crossed the old steel bridge over the river. At the traffic light on the Pennsylvania side of the bridge, he looked in his side-view mirrors and saw two men, maybe three, get out of their car and run up to either side of his car. The angle of his mirror prevented him from seeing their faces and in a second they were next to his window.

"You're under arrest!" one of the men said.

He turned fearfully and saw it was Chuck. In the other window, he saw Teddy's and Liz's faces.

"Yo!" Henry said. "What are you guys doin' here?"

"Did you get in a fight with a lawnmower?" Teddy asked. He reached over and grabbed the back of Henry's head.

They went to the diner on Bridge Street in Morrisville.

"I told you a while back," Chuck said. "I said if you ever need anything, use us."

"Yeah, of course. But I don't need anything. I mean, I got everything."

"To say we're all really concerned about you is an understatement," Teddy said.

"You shouldn't be worried at all, guys. I'm fine."

"You ran away from home!" Liz said.

"Listen." Teddy grabbed Henry's arm to make sure he was paying attention. "I've been through all this shit and believe me, I know exactly what you're going through."

Henry turned down to his food. "Why are you guys teaming up on me?"

"It's called looking out for our brother" Chuck said. "Put yourself in our shoes for a second."

"It's not. It's not like that. Stop worrying already. I'll be fine. Me and Esther are good together."

"Well, will you call us if you need something?" Liz asked.

"I won't need anything. I'm ready to take on whatever life throws at me."

Henry did more job searching in Pennsylvania that day but still found nothing.

CHAPTER 11

A week later, Henry sat in the Toyota out front of the apartment, counting his money—five dollars. As he climbed the steps to the apartment, Esther appeared at the top. "I've been looking for you," she said. "I have to tell you something." She saw a defeated look on his face and reached for his hand.

He walked past her. "I have to tell you something, too."

She followed him into the bedroom and eased onto the bed as he stood watching her.

"I lost—," he began to say. But Willy passed the bedroom so Henry threw the door shut. "I lost my job."

She stared at him.

"I lost my job," he repeated.

"I heard. I was just processing it. Just today?"

"Last week."

"Last week!? Why are you just telling me now?"

"I tried to tell you the other day...remember, when we were in the bathroom? But then I just... I wanted to surprise you and have another job lined up before I even told you."

"That's a big let-down."

"I lost my job," Henry said, defensively. "I'm sorry."

"I'm not talking about you losing the job. I'm talking about you not communicating with me, and not trusting me."

"I'm sorry," he sat on the bed with her. "I'll try harder."

"I'm not going to ruin this moment by lecturing you."

"Ruin what moment?" he asked.

"I'll tell you in a second. But, you have to promise me something."

"Okay?"

"You have to promise me that from this point forward you will always, always trust me and communicate with me."

"I promise." He put his hand on his heart.

"You promise me what?"

"I promise that I'll always trust you and communicate with you."

She smiled. "Thank you. So what happened at work?"

"Jesus. I feel like such an asshole," he said. He put his arm around her. He told her about the incident with Mr. Penn and the Jaguar.

She laughed at him. "Yeah, that was stupid Henry."

"Believe me I know!"

"You need to find another job now." She leaned into him.

"I've been looking. I'll find something. So what did you have to tell me?" he asked.

She kissed him on the cheek. "This is big news," she said.

"Big... big...? Tell me!"

She lifted her shirt, grabbed his hand and spread his fingers across her belly.

He looked in her eyes and saw them soft and teary.

"I'm pregnant," she said.

He stared at her—speechless. And, just when she expected he would embrace her, he withdrew his hand and tumbled out of the bed, falling onto the floor.

She reached for him as he got up, but he evaded her. When he went for the door he slammed into it, thinking it would open out. Then he pulled it open and darted out of the room.

Willy, who was in the hall listening to their conversation, watched Henry run past and go down the steps to leave. Willy ran into the kitchen, opened the cabinet under the sink, and grabbed a bottle of rum. He ran outside after Henry.

Henry was walking quickly down Hamilton Avenue in the dusk when Willy caught up and started walking along with him. When they arrived at Hudson Street, Willy nudged Henry to turn. Henry shot him a nasty look.

"Come on, brotha," Willy said. "Come with me."

Henry followed. They walked down to Tyler Street and turned down the alley next to the rundown house they had gone in the week before.

In the house, Henry sat on the chair across from the mattress on the floor. "Don't punch me in the fucking head again."

Willy took the cap off the bottle of rum and handed it to Henry. Henry took a long drink and gagged a bit. He shook it off and handed the bottle back to Willy.

Willy took a small sip of the rum. "So you gonna be the man?" he asked.

"How do I *be the man*?

"By drivin' for me." Willy rubbed his fingers together. "And earnin' some quick cash."

"I told you before, it's not for me."

Willy nodded and paced. "Well it sounds like you need some money."

"You were listening to our conversation?"

"I overheard the conversation, yes. Listen Kreiser, you're gonna get there eventually, to that moment when you realize that workin' for $5.15 an hour is a disgrace."

"I was making $5.75 at the factory."

"You *was*," Willy tapped Henry on the shoulder with the bottle of rum. "But now you unemployed."

Henry grabbed the bottle back and took another drink.

"So," Willy continued, "I suggest you finally admit to where you're goin'."

Henry thought about it for a long moment. "What's involved?" he asked.

"Just drivin'. Listen, this is not for just anybody but this *is* for you. I'm sure of it."

"Shut up." Henry was loosening up from the two big gulps of rum.

"I'm serious. I'm not just tellin' you this shit because I

need your help. I'm tellin' you because I know you'll be fuckin' good at it. You're serious and straight forward now. No fuckin' around. It's so simple for a guy like you. You're just gonna be a driver."

"Yeah, sounds easy enough I guess," Henry said, "but guns and jail don't sound like no fun to me."

"Brotha, it's almost impossible for you to get busted. And everybody involved is checked out."

"Nah man. Nah. I can't ever get involved in something like that." Henry slouched down in the chair.

"Come on. Tell you what. Don't give me a definite answer yet. But, why don't you drive me over to do my first pickup tomorrow morning? It's a trial run for me and can be a trial run for you. If you don't want to continue after tomorrow I'll never bug you about it again."

"Over where?"

"Like I told you, West side of Trenton—ten minutes from here."

Henry smiled for a second, but then became serious all of a sudden. "Nah. No thanks." He got up to leave. "I gotta go home and talk to Esther."

Willy punched at Henry but stopped short. Henry flinched then jumped up and punched back. They went toe to toe for a couple seconds, sparring without making contact, and then Willy stopped. "Come on man. Just take me over there tomorrow. You'll have two benjamins in your pocket by nine a.m."

Henry didn't reply.

"Good," Willy said. "We'll leave at seven in the morning." He handed Henry the bottle of rum.

Henry drank in big long gulps.

"Settle down," Willy said.

Henry drank more and faster, then sat back and watched as Willy started running around the house—taking some pots and pans to the basement and moving a cabinet to block the front door. Within twenty minutes, Henry was drunk and losing a clear sense of where he was. When he tried to get up from the couch, he stumbled and half-intentionally fell onto the bed where he quickly passed out.

Willy was in and out of the house that evening. Henry woke occasionally with bed spins. At one point he got up, feeling queasy, and glanced at his surroundings. It was dark now and a strip of silver streetlight crossed the ceiling of the room from a side window of the house. A deep uneasiness grumbled in his belly. He ran into the front room and searched around. He saw a staircase, so he scrambled up. At the top, he darted into a bathroom and kneeled down at the filthy toilet just in time to let go. He vomited repeatedly.

After several minutes the queasiness subsided, so he drank water from the spigot in the bathtub. Then, he stumbled through the dark hallway to the next room, where another mattress was on the floor. He flopped down on it and passed out again.

He tossed and turned throughout the night. Doors opened and closed several times in the adjacent rooms. He was half awake when he sensed somebody watching. He sat up in bed and looked to the hallway where he saw a teenage black girl in a white tube dress with a fat, white man in slacks and a button down shirt. The odd couple moved down the hallway before Henry could make sense of anything. He fell back asleep. A bit later, he woke to the sound of grunting and moaning—the fat man. There was a steady pounding on a wall. The noises crescendoed and then stopped suddenly.

"Get off me," he heard the girl demand.

Doors opened and closed again. Then a sweet smell of burning rubber reached Henry's nose. He slept again. Henry slept for no more than an hour when a truck moving on the street outside woke him. He popped up. His head spun and his mouth and throat were parched and scratchy. Out in the hallway he snuck down to the next room, where the door was ajar. He saw the girl sprawled across the bed, with the tube dress bunched around her waist. She was fully exposed from the waist down except for one knee which had a sheet lying across it. A makeshift pipe of tinfoil lay on the floor next to a lighter. Henry pulled the door shut and went downstairs. Willy was asleep on the mattress in the middle room when Henry snuck past and escaped out the back door.

The sunrise was just arriving and a dawn breeze blew trash around a wild patch of grass in a broken sidewalk. He walked from Tyler Street down to the train station. Inside, working men in blue shirts drank coffee and watched the arrivals and departures board—rushing off for a train when Henry arrived. He went to the bathroom and washed his face. He took his bandanna off and tucked the gold chain into his shirt.

Outside of the station he stood at a railing, looking into a wooded area that sat between the railroad tracks and a row of homes. He was tired and nervous and the sound of a car passing on the road nearby startled him. *How could I ever?*, he thought. *How could I ever be a father?* He saw a path into the wooded area strewn with beer bottles and trash. Again, a car driving on the road nearby startled him, so he jumped over the railing, onto the path and into the woods. It was cool, damp and dark on the path. A train passed on the tracks nearby—its brakes scraping and hissing. Then something, or someone, moved suddenly in the underbrush, so Henry ran away quickly. He emerged from the wooded area onto Greenwood Avenue, and then passed in front of the huge, empty Trenton Central High School. The roads were filling up with cars and trucks. When he got onto Hamilton Avenue his pace increased. He went directly to Esther's house.

Henry pulled his keys out and was about to enter the apartment, when he heard somebody call him from a block away. He saw Willy running up the street. "Kreiser! Where you goin'?"

"I'm goin' in to talk to my girl!"

"What!?" Willy arrived quickly.

"You heard me."

Willy shoved Henry back from the door. "You told me you was gonna take me to the west side."

"No I didn't!" Henry motioned as if he was going to shove Willy back but he stopped, and instead he searched through his keys and approached the door again.

Willy grabbed Henry's arm and pulled him violently away. "Let's go Kreiser. Don't let your brotha down right now. I need to get over there in thirty minutes or I'm fucked. They waitin' on me."

Henry shook off Willy's tight grip. "Willy! Would you stop this fuckin' shit?"

Willy stood back.

Henry approached him. "I told you," he said with a hushed tone. "I don't want to have anything to do with it."

"But, Kreiser, you said you would take me. Now, I'm gonna lose a major opportunity."

"When did I say I would take you?"

"Last night, when you started drinkin' the rum."

Henry thought to himself for a moment. "I said I would take you?"

"Yeah man. And I depended on you. I would have taken another ride over there."

"I always feel like you're trying to manipulate me Willy."

"Well, you're wrong about that, man. I just wanted to give you an opportunity. You make your own fuckin' decisions. Right? And last night you made your own decision when you told me you would take me over there. So, I canceled the other ride I had setup. Now you gotta take me. It's the only right thing to do."

Henry let out a long sigh.

"Come on." Willy knocked his shoulder into Henry's. "You'll be back before Esther even wakes up."

Henry searched his eyes. "What do I gotta do?"

"Just take me to the west side. I run in and make the pick-up and we leave. You ain't even gonna be there when the deal goes down. Then I give you two hundred dollars."

Henry shrugged and shook his head. They approached his car and got in.

"What street?" Henry asked as he started the car.

"Perry. Take Perry to Bank." Willy looked at Henry. "Where's your bandanna and gold chain?"

"I'm not wearing 'em."

"Why?" Willy asked. "That was a good look."

"Just because." He drove off quickly.

As they crossed through the downtown area, Willy stared out the window. He began mumbling to himself as he pulled something from his waist band. Henry glanced over and saw the pistol. Then Willy pulled out a bundle of cash. Henry swerved suddenly, almost losing control.

"Keep your fucking eyes on the road, Kreiser. If we get pulled over I'm gonna shoot your dumb ass."

Henry continued to watch Willy out of the corner of his eye. Willy slipped the gun between the seat and the emergency brake. "Listen, Kreiser," he said, turning his attention to Henry.

"Yeah?"

"When I get out of this car I need to know that you got my back."

Henry glanced over and saw Willy's eyes dead serious. "What do you mean?" Henry asked.

"I mean a lot of different things can happen. So, if something is not goin' so good I need to know that you're gonna try to help me out."

"Aw man!" Henry smacked the steering wheel. He became nervous suddenly. "I thought you said this was gonna be easy."

"Relax. It is, I just need to know that you rock solid. You my brotha and I know that I got your back no matter what. So, I wanna know you got mine."

Henry glanced over at Willy a few more times. He stopped at a red light and looked down at the gun next to the seat. "Yeah, of course I got your back, but I—"

"Good," Willy cut him off. "I thought so."

They continued across Trenton. Perry Street curved and changed names twice. "There," Willy said, as they entered a neighborhood full of abandon homes. "Turn there." They turned onto the narrow Kater Street. They passed a few row homes, and then turned onto another larger road. When they reached an expansive, old Victorian style house with bars on all of the windows, Willy motioned for Henry to stop the car. Henry glanced at the gun beside the seat nervously and watched Willy jump out.

"Five minutes," Willy said, darting over to the side yard of the big house.

A few cars drove by as ten minutes passed. Henry watched an old black lady pass by on the sidewalk. Then two young kids carrying school books walked across the street up ahead of him. A few minutes later, a royal blue Ford Escort parked in front of Henry's Toyota, and an older white lady in a nurse's uniform got out. He watched the nurse open the hatchback and pull out a big plastic box with a handle. She glanced at Henry and gave a polite smile, and then crossed the street with the box. She climbed up the front steps of a nearby house.

Henry remembered the pistol, so he pulled it out of its hiding place next to the seat. Looking around cautiously, to make sure nobody was watching, he examined the pistol in his hand. He kept the barrel pointed at the floor. He touched the trigger and saw the safety lock next to it. In that same moment, he saw something move in his rearview mirror and tensed up. He watched a black van pull to a stop, about fifty yards behind his car. He kept his eyes on the rearview mirror as the van sat there for several minutes. Then he tensed again when two men suddenly jumped out of the side of the van—white men wearing jeans and black windbreakers and carrying rifles. The men darted into an alley between two houses.

Henry started the car and pulled forward a few feet—so he could see up the alley where Willy went. There was nobody in sight at first. But then, Henry saw the two men in windbreakers cross pass the backside of the same alley. Henry began to breathe heavily and realized the pistol was sitting on his lap. He dropped it on the floor and slowly pulled his car past the blue Ford Escort.

When he reached the intersection about twenty yards further, he hit the gas pedal hard. But as the Toyota lunged forward, he had to slam the brakes immediately. An unmarked police car screeched to a stop in front of him. He was stunned. Two more men in black windbreakers with badges printed on their chests jumped out. One of them held an assault weapon and the other had his handgun drawn. The officer with the handgun stopped next to Henry's car, pointing his gun toward the ground, as the other officer ran back into the side yard of the house.

"Window down!" the officer called.

Henry rolled down his window.

The officer's radio crackled as somebody on the other end shouted things Henry couldn't understand. Then the officer freed up a hand and grabbed the radio. "White male, late teens, blond hair sort of... uh..." the officer took a closer look at Henry. "..sort of high on the top." Then he directed a question at Henry. "What's your name?"

"Henry Kreiser," Henry responded nervously. He felt a drip of sweat roll down his back. With his foot he found the pistol on the floor and slowly nudged it back underneath the seat.

"What are you doing here?"

Henry looked in the rearview mirror and saw the nurse's blue Ford Escort. He didn't know what to say.

"What are you doing here!?" the officer asked again.

"I uh... I just dropped off my grandmother. She's a nurse. Her client lives right back there."

The officer called on his radio again. "He dropped the nurse off."

The voice on the other end crackled more clearly, "I thought they said the nurse came in the Ford."

The officer stepped closer to Henry's window and started to look around inside of the car. "Did you see somebody pull up in the Ford Escort behind your vehicle?" the officer asked Henry.

Henry looked back in the rearview mirror again. "That one back there?"

The officer nodded.

"Yeah," Henry said. "Some black kid."

"Turn off your car."

Henry turned it off and watched in his side-view mirror as the officer moved to the back of the Toyota, holstered his gun, and pulled out a pad of paper and pen. Before he started writing, though, a gunshot popped off at the house. The officer dropped the pen. Then, another shot was fired and he dropped the pad of paper. Henry saw the officer pull his gun back out. "Stay here!" he shouted to Henry, before running off to the house.

Henry heard yelling. "Inside! Back away! Down!" He started the Toyota and pulled slowly around the unmarked patrol car. When he got out onto the cross street, he heard two more shots, so he drove off quickly. After turning the next corner, though, he slammed his brakes yet again. "Fuck!" he yelled. He punched the dashboard. He put the car in neutral and got out.

He could see, through an alley way, to the backside of the same big Victorian house that Willy had entered.

"Will!" Henry yelled. "Willy!" Henry approached a couple of steps to get a closer look, when saw an officer tucked tight against the house with his pistol drawn. Henry froze for a second, then swung around and quickly jumped back in the Toyota. He sat there for a second, thinking. He looked back up the alley and rolled down the passenger side window. "Willy!" he yelled. "Uh... I gotta run... so..." He hit the gas and sped away with a screech. As he shot through the next red light, he heard one more gun shot.

He drove fast and blew through red lights for nearly five minutes before slowing down and taking deep, long breaths. He found himself among the state buildings in downtown Trenton. A stream of office workers in suits and dresses, many holding their morning coffee in hand, entered the glass and mirror state buildings.

Henry drove to the old steel bridge that led to Pennsylvania. As he sat at a red light, he touched one hand with the other, finding his palms were sopped in sweat. He felt moisture dripping down his back. He used his collar to wipe sweat from the back of his head. He tensed for a second when a police car passed on the road in front of him. His thoughts were jumbled and he had no clarity whatsoever. *Fuckin' shit*, he thought. *Fuckin' fuckin' motherfuckin' shit.* He punched the dashboard and shook the steering wheel. *Fuck!* When the light turned green, he pulled across the bridge.

In Pennsylvania, he drove around slowly, not quite knowing where to go. He drove in the direction of Kate's house in Levittown, but when he came to her street he drove past it. He circled back again to her street, and even put his turn signal on. But again, he drove past without turning down her street.

Then he drove over to Truman High School and stopped in front. The school sign read, "Get Ready For School. Welcome The Class of 1989". He sighed as he looked at the sign. But then he really began to feel the rum headache and scratchy thirst in his throat, so he pulled off.

At the Seven-Eleven on Route 13 he sat in the car and searched through his wallet—five dollars. He looked at the fuel indicator needle, seeing it was near empty. He found a quarter in the console of the car, so he took it and went to the pay phone.

There was no answer when he called Kate's house but her answering machine picked up. "Hey," he said, after the beep, "just calling to say hi and stuff. I just want to... uh... just say... uh... I have good news... So, gimme a call when you get a chance. Say hi to everybody for me." He left the phone number for Esther's house, and then went into the store. He bought a bottle of Gatorade and a two-pack of Tylenol.

As he continued driving he took the two Tylenols and drank the Gatorade quickly in big long gulps. He drove down to the quaint riverfront in Bristol and sat, watching the river from his car window. He put his seat back and closed his eyes, feeling a growing sense of calm as the Gatorade and Tylenol eased into his body. In a moment he was asleep.

He woke more than an hour later as a breeze blew through the car and pushed a piece of paper from the dashboard to the floor between his feet. Then he suddenly remembered the pistol, so he put his seat up, reached down under the seat, and felt the barrel. He drove off again immediately.

After searching and turning around a couple of times in Tullytown, he found the road that led to the trash dump. The large hill loomed up ahead. When he got to the entrance he saw a man padlocking the gate with his truck stopped nearby, so Henry drove past the entrance, pulled over a short distance down the road, and watched in his rearview mirror. When the truck pulled away, Henry went back and turned his car into the entrance—looking along the length of chain link fence for a way inside. A few dozen yards down the fence he saw a cat scurry through a gap at the bottom. He turned off the car and thought to himself for a moment. Then he grabbed the gun from under his seat, shoved it in his pants, and got out of the car.

At the spot where he had seen the cat enter, Henry was able to push the fence up enough to squeeze through the dirt underneath it and enter. As he brushed the dirt off his shirt, he glanced around the hill. One half of the dump site was ripped apart and had bulldozers and dump trucks parked on it, while the other half was pleasantly landscaped with fresh, young trees and grass. He approached the area that was landscaped and began climbing the hill. He recalled the morning he ran away from Kate's house, rode his bicycle through this area, and watched the seagulls swooping up and down. When he got to the top of the hill, he stepped into the late afternoon sunlight. He was standing in rich green grass nearly ankle high. He searched the surrounding areas from his high vantage point and recognized the city streets of Trenton across the river. He saw sprawling Levittown in the opposite direction. But in every other direction, towns and developments, in both Pennsylvania and New Jersey, stretched off as far as he could see—none of which were familiar to him. Clouds were absent, save for one or two puffs off near the horizon. He sat down on the grass and lay back to look at the sky. He inhaled deeply, surprised that, despite being at a trash dump, he only smelled fresh air. Wind blew the grass against his cheek. It tickled the side of his head. He swatted at the grass, as if it was a bug, and sat up. When he did, he heard a car driving on the road out in front of the dump, so he searched the full length of the road and found it. It was Byron's car—the Subaru Brat. He watched Byron speed down the road then skid to a stop near the entrance of the dump, behind the Toyota. Byron got out of the Subaru and looked in the windows of Henry's car, and then at the gate of the dump. When he got back in the Subaru he pulled away slowly, looking around. And then, at the end of the road, he sped off again.

Henry lay back on the grass, feeling the warmth of the sun on one side of his face. He felt the metal barrel of the pistol against his thigh, so he pulled it out of his waistband. As he lay there, he examined the gun in his hands. He pointed it to the sky, aiming for a high-flying bird and putting his finger on the trigger. And then, he aimed at another bird and touched the trigger again.

He took a deep breath and gave a long exhale, and laid the gun down in the grass. His thoughts were still jumbled but he daydreamed. Images moved through his mind as a feeling—warm and new—stirred inside of him. He imagined sunny and beautiful places just like the place he was in at that moment. And then he saw friendly, happy people that loved and hugged each other. There was a cow and a rollercoaster and a church. There was a woman embracing a naked infant in her arms, as she waded into ocean waves. He saw the arrivals and departures sign from Trenton train station as it flipped through the list of cities.

His daydream was interrupted by the sound of a car passing on the road again. He sat up and saw Byron returning in the Subaru followed by another car; Kate's Pontiac sedan. Both of the cars stopped next to Henry's at the entrance. When Henry took a closer look he saw the cars had additional passengers that started to step out one by one. Henry stood now and walked a few steps closer. In addition to Byron and Kate, there was Teddy, Liz, Chuck and Veronica. Then, Esther emerged. He saw Esther shake Teddy's hand and then Chuck's, as if they were meeting for the first time. After chatting, they looked in the Toyota then began scanning the high dump hill.

Henry laughed. *"Oh my God. What are they all doing here?"* he thought. He felt his eyes well up and a tear ran down his cheek. He wiped the tear on his sleeve then brushed a few blades of grass from the top of his hair. He held his hands high in the air. "I'm here!" he yelled. Then, just as he uttered those words, and his voice echoed back, Esther's gaze fell on Henry. She saw him standing on the crest of the hill and motioned for the attention of the others. When they all waved to him, he waved back and started down the hill.

GREG KIESER was born in Langhorne, Pennsylvania in 1970. He currently resides in Brooklyn, New York.

AMERICAN SPAZ THE NOVEL, his first published work, is autobiographical fiction and chronicles a decade of his life – from 7 to 17 years old – during which time he lost both parents, moved from place to place, and did whatever he needed to do to survive. As the youngest of six children he had many opportunities, during that decade, to rely on, and sometimes reject, the love of family.

www.ingramcontent.com/pod-product-compliance
Lightning Source LLC
Chambersburg PA
CBHW071958290426
44109CB00018B/2060